Assemblies
Through tl

Edited by Gordon Lamont

Published in Great Britain in 2003 by
Society for Promoting Christian Knowledge
Holy Trinity Church
Marylebone Road
London NW1 4DU

British Library Cataloguing-in-Publication Data

A catalogue record for this book
is available from the British Library

ISBN 0-281-05567-X

10 9 8 7 6 5 4 3 2 1

Typeset by Wilmaset Ltd, Birkenhead, Wirral
Printed in Great Britain by
The Cromwell Press, Trowbridge, Wilts

Contents

Introduction

Assemblies! – you love them or hate them, often at the same time. Whatever your faith background, whether committed believer, seeker, agnostic or committed atheist, along with most people you probably value the idea of a common celebration, a time to be together and think together. In the abstract there's a lot to be said for assemblies, but the practicality of coming up with something fresh day after day, week after week – well, that's a different matter. Through the creation of the assemblies website – www.assemblies.org.uk – and through the first *Assemblies Resource Book*, SPCK aimed to support busy teachers and ministers as they faced that regular question and its accompanying sinking feeling – what shall I do for assembly today?

The website, which was launched in autumn 1999, aims to offer support with ideas that can be picked up and used immediately or, more commonly, adapted to fit your school's situation and needs.

One of the great joys of the site is the way that it has taken on a life of its own. Assemblies are now written, almost exclusively, by users. These are ordinary teachers and ministers who want to share their assembly experiences through the website. This creation of a virtual and self-sustaining community is the Holy Grail of web producers, and if you add to it the practical outcomes – real assemblies being delivered in real school halls to, yes, real children across the country – then you have a web success story on a grand scale. We don't know how many children experience assemblies from the site, but we do know that it is an awfully big number – certainly a million in any month, sometimes perhaps as many as a million a week.

With these numbers accessing the site and using its offerings you could be forgiven for thinking that a book is unnecessary – isn't it old technology, superseded by the web site itself with its easy navigation and excellent search facility? Apparently not, as sales of the first *Assemblies Resource Book* have demonstrated. It appears that our users want both web resources and printed resources, and so we are pleased to offer this new collection of the best of recent postings on the website.

This time we have presented the assemblies under four headings: Christian Festivals and Themes, Stories from the Bible, Festivals of World Religions, and Other Themes. This last section contains mostly PSE and Citizenship assemblies. We recognize that the offerings are far from exhaustive. The World Religions section can only skim the surface of the many festivals and celebrations available; neither is the Christian Festivals and Themes section complete. The website is a continuing and evolving platform and this book can only represent a snapshot of some of the available offerings.

Although we indicate on the assemblies themselves which level the writer intended they be suitable for, we have not organized them by Key Stage, as we do not wish to exclude the imaginative adaptation that takes an idea for year 5 and makes it accessible for year 3. As usual our ethos is to trust the professionals, so read on, adapt and present in your own style. We hope you and the children enjoy the experience.

GORDON LAMONT

Editor, www.assemblies.org.uk

Christian Festivals and Themes

THE FLYING PIZZA – A HARVEST ASSEMBLY

By the Revd Alan M. Barker

Suitable for Whole School

 ### Aim

To appreciate the scale of global food production and the concept of 'food miles'.

 ### Preparation and materials

- Pizza ingredients: a pizza base, tomato puree or pasta sauce, tuna fish chunks, sliced pineapple, sliced red pepper, sliced mushrooms, grated or mozzarella cheese, pepper grinder containing black peppercorns, and a pizza box.
- Pieces of card to display 'food miles' (see 2. below).
- *Optional*: For 3. below, children could prepare examples of locally bought but globally produced food.

 ### Assembly

1. Explain that when you're feeling hungry it's sometimes a treat to send out for a pizza. Remind the children of the distance to the local pizza take-away – for many people a pizza can be cooked and delivered in a short time.
2. Introduce the idea that the ingredients of a pizza may have travelled far further. Explain by inviting a group of children to help place toppings on the prepared pizza base. Display the miles that the different ingredients have travelled. (Distances are approximate.)

   Flour from North America – 5,400 miles (8,600 km)
   Tomatoes from Italy – 1,000 miles (1,600 km)
   Tuna fish from Mauritius – 5,600 miles (9,000 km)

Pineapples grown and harvested in Kenya – 4,500 miles (7,200 km)

Peppers grown in Dutch glasshouses – 400 miles (640 km)

Mushrooms grown in the United Kingdom but transported from the growers to your supermarket – 200 miles (320 km)

Black pepper from India – 5,000 miles (8,000 km)

Mozzarella cheese, also from Italy – 1,000 miles (1,600 km)

So the pizza that is delivered from 'just around the corner' has in fact flown an incredible distance of 23,000 miles (37,000 km) around the world.

3. Remind the children that much of the food we take for granted has been produced in other parts of the world, travelling great distances to our plates. Encourage them to look at the labels of tins and packets as they shop. A group of children may present other examples of locally bought but globally produced food, e.g. tea, coffee, fruit.

    Point out that on average vegetables travel 600 miles (950 km) to your supermarket, some by plane, and all by lorry.

4. For KS2 children, introduce the concept of 'food miles' – the distance food is transported from producers to consumers (those who buy and eat it). Modern transport enables us to enjoy a world of food on our doorstep. The down side of this, however, is that much fuel is burned by the food industry, at a cost both to consumers and to the environment. Also, those who are food producers do not always receive fair prices from customers on the other side of the world.

5. Encourage everyone to use the occasion of a Harvest celebration to think about the varied origins of our food and the benefits and disadvantages of food that 'travels miles'.

6. Cook and enjoy the pizza!

 Time for reflection

Bible link: Deuteronomy 8.7–11. The people of the Old Testament were warned not to take for granted the ability of the earth to grow food. There is always the danger that with plentiful food supplies we don't stop to think how much we depend on others.

Creator God,
thank you for food from around the world
and for the different tastes that we enjoy.
Help us to use the resources of the earth wisely and well,
to the benefit of all peoples.
Amen.

 Song

'Lord of the harvest' (*Come and Praise*, 133)

REMEMBERING TOGETHER

By the Revd Alan M. Barker

Suitable for KS2

Aim

To appreciate the importance of shared memories and Armistice Day. *Bible link*: Matthew 5.3–10 (Jesus' famous sayings called the Beatitudes help us to remember how happiness can be found and shared).

Preparation and materials

● You will need a 'memory display' consisting of a British Legion poppy and other items associated with memory, e.g. a photograph, a diary, an appointments calendar, a fridge magnet, a Post-it note, a video, a knotted handkerchief, an electronic organizer, a floppy disk, a newspaper clipping, a war-time medal. All the items need to be arranged so that they are clearly visible to all the children, but to begin with they are carefully covered with a sheet.

Assembly

1. Tell the children that you are going to test their memory. Show the objects in the memory display for just a short while. Ask one child to recall as many as they can, while you compile a list of things remembered. Explain that he or she will probably need the help of others to remember everything – ask other children to help until the list is completed.

2. Point out that the children had to help one another to remember, and that the items displayed were all associated with memory. Talk about some of the items, highlighting their significance. Some help us to remember and plan for future events. Others assist us to remember past events and

people. Who keeps a diary or uses an electronic organizer . . . or a scrap-book?

3. What special times and experiences do the children recall? We can all remember both happy and sad experiences. Remembering helps us to learn from the past and to plan for the future. The sharing of memories is an important part of family, school, and community life.

4. Focus on the poppy and explain that it helps us to remember those who lost their lives or were injured in wartime. The Poppy Day Appeal, organized by the Royal British Legion, helps those ex-servicemen and women who continue to suffer as a result of wartime injuries, and it also helps their families.

   Explain that the poppy was chosen as an emblem after the First World War (1914–18). Thousands of soldiers fought in France and many lives were lost in trench warfare. (A photograph might help everyone to understand.) Each summer poppies grew in the soil churned up by the fighting and their colour spoke of the blood which had been shed. War memorials in almost every town and village list the names of those killed, and so help us to remember how the war brought sadness and disruption to so many homes. Refer to a local war memorial and, if appropriate, the phrase 'Lest we forget'.

5. Conclude by talking about the silence observed at 11 a.m. on Armistice Day, 11 November, and in church services on Remembrance Sunday. It is a way of remembering not only past events but also the suffering that war continues to bring to the world today. Some will remember heroes, others will mourn friends whose lives have been lost. It's important that in this way we help one another to remember. The sharing of memories strengthens our community life. If appropriate, build a time of silence for this purpose into the reflection below.

Time for reflection

Invite the children to quietly remember a happy time and to be thankful for it. Ask them to recall a difficult time and to remember friends who helped. Ask them to remember others in need of help because of the suffering caused by war.

Lord God,
We thank you for the gift of memories that we can share
together.
Help us not to forget the feelings of others.
May we heal painful memories through kindness
and create better, happier, memories for tomorrow.
Amen.

 Song

'Make me a channel of your peace' (*Come and Praise*, 147)

GETTING STIRRED UP!

By *the Revd Alan M. Barker*

Suitable for Whole School

Aim

To begin to 'get ready' for Christmas by reflecting how to make a better world. For the week preceding Advent.

Preparation and materials

- Ask ten children to help you.
- A large clear pyrex bowl and mixing spoon, and the following ingredients weighed into separate freezer bags: 3 oz (85 g) plain flour; 3 oz (85 g) suet; 4 oz (110 g) dark brown sugar; ½ tsp baking powder with ½ tsp mixed spice; ½ oz (15 g) flaked almonds; 4 oz (110 g) raisins; 4 oz (110 g) sultanas; 6 oz (170 g) currants; 2 oz (55 g) mixed peel; 2 medium eggs (best broken into a small storage container).
- The Collect (short prayer) for Stir-up Sunday on an OHP or flip-chart: 'Stir up, O Lord, the wills of your faithful people: that richly bearing the fruit of good works, they may by you be richly rewarded; through Jesus Christ our Lord.'

Assembly

1. Explain that the season of Advent begins on four Sundays before Christmas. It's a time to 'get ready' for Christmas. The Sunday before Advent is traditionally known as 'Stir-up' Sunday. It's the time of year when Christmas puddings are made so that they have time to 'steep' (i.e. all the juices and flavours mix together and grow) before Christmas.
2. Ask the children if they would like to make a pudding – here, now in assembly. Would they really? When the response is sufficiently enthusiastic, comment that the idea seems to have really got them stirred-up!

3. Introduce the ingredients one by one, in the order that they are listed. Give one to each volunteer. There could be the opportunity to explore the different textures and aromas. Ask each helper first to add their ingredient to the bowl, and then to stir them together. While they are doing this invite them to close their eyes and secretly make a wish. Traditionally, all the members of a household would take a turn at stirring in order to do this.

4. When the mixture is complete (adding the eggs often causes a stir!), explain that there is a special prayer associated with Stir-up Sunday. Display the prayer and point out that the words 'stir up', 'fruit', 'good' and 'richly' could refer to making a pudding. In fact, the prayer is about making the most of life. How ready (stirred-up) are we to take positive action to help everyone enjoy life more?

5. Ask the children to suggest different positive actions ('good works') to 'enrich' the lives of others and make a better world, e.g. supporting the Blue Peter Christmas Appeal or the BBC Children in Need Appeal; befriending those who are new to the school; visiting elderly relatives; praying for peace; caring for the environment. The stirring spoon could be passed to individual children to hold as they make their suggestions.

6. Sum up by reflecting that getting ready for Christmas isn't just a matter of preparing food. It's also important that we are stirred up and ready to act upon our deepest wishes and prayers for others. But note that the pudding mixture must now be steamed for at least 8 hours, and that in the same way many of the changes we long for may take time!

 Time for reflection

Read together the Collect for Stir-up Sunday or use the following prayer:

Lord God,
we thank you for the excitement of starting to get ready for Christmas.
In all of our Advent preparations, stir up our imagination

and help us to be more ready to enrich the lives of others
and to make a better world.
Amen.

 Song

'Christmas, Christmas' (*Come and Praise*, 122)

ADVENT

By Gordon and Ronni Lamont

Suitable for Whole School

 Aim

To introduce and explore the season of Advent.

 Preparation and materials

- Collect some different Advent calendars and candles. Scour the local shops/charity shops and catalogues. Try to get the following:
  - A 'branded' young child's calendar, such as a Thomas the Tank Engine with chocolates type – one with no religious significance at all.
  - A traditional nativity scene calendar with pictures.
  - A calendar with another culture theme – Christian Aid usually produces one showing how different cultures celebrate the season.
  - A fabric or embroidered calendar. Ask around and you may be able to find a homemade one.
  - At least one Advent candle. Ideally try to get one of the ball type ones (each day has a small ball candle, and you pull them through to sit on the candlestick day by day), but any Advent candle will do.
- Arrange the calendars and candles attractively, so the children can see them all.

 Assembly

1. Ask the children what these things are. What are they for? Who's got one at home? Ask them what sort they have. Many will only know the Thomas with chocolates type. Go through the different types, showing the children how they work. Ask

individual children to open the doors on the calendars, and light the candle(s) if time allows, or light them yourself.

2. Explain that the calendars help us to wait, and expect. What are we waiting for? What happened on the first Christmas day?

3. When we have special visitors, what do we do before they come? We clean up, and get ourselves ready. We think about the visitors and look forward to their arrival. This is the meaning of Advent – arrival. Advent is a time to prepare ourselves – to get ready. Some people like to have less to eat during Advent, so that when Christmas comes, they can really appreciate the food and the fun. Who are we getting ready for? Who are we expecting to arrive?

4. Ask the children to think to themselves, in a time of quiet, about what they would put behind the windows of an Advent calendar. What would they choose to represent this special time of year? Ask for suggestions. Choose about five of the most appropriate to be represented in still pictures at the front of the hall.

5. The still pictures are made by children holding a position, like a photograph. This can be the person who suggested the idea on their own, or with a friend if the still picture needs more than one person. Some ideas for Advent still pictures: buying presents for family and friends (child and shop assistant); lighting a candle; opening a door on the Advent calendar. But, of course, be ready for more idiosyncratic ideas from the children.(If this 'living Advent calendar' is a success, you could reprise the idea at assemblies leading up to Christmas with children working out still pictures in advance.)

 ## Time for reflection

Look at the candle(s), and think about being ready for Christmas – the birthday of Jesus and a time of celebration and fun.

Think of all the preparations that will be made at home: the food, the tree, the presents. How can you help to make Advent a really good time at home?

Think of everything special that happens at school at this

time of year. How can you help to make Advent a really good
time at school?

 Song

'Come and praise the Lord our King' (*Come and Praise*, 21)

THE LEGEND OF ST BONIFACE

By the Revd Alan M. Barker

Suitable for KS2

Aim

To reflect upon experiences of fear and to appreciate the significance of the 'Christmas tree'.

Preparation and materials

- A miniature Christmas tree growing in a pot, or a Christmas tree decoration.
- Read through the story of St Boniface below so you can tell it with feeling and imagination.
- The story could be told by a narrator and mimed by a group of children.

Assembly

1. Ask whether any of the children will have a Christmas tree in their homes at Christmas time. Is it a real one? What are the advantages and disadvantages of having a 'real' tree? The aroma and appearance of a real tree are attractive. However, they can drop their needles and often die after Christmas because their roots have been cut.

2. Reflect that while the children are attracted to one small tree, many big trees growing together in a forest can sometimes seem frightening – especially when they are dark and shadowy. Are the children ever frightened of shadows?

   Say that a long time ago some people were especially frightened of large and ancient trees. They thought that powerful spirits lived within them. Rituals were performed to please the spirits so they wouldn't harm anyone. Invite the children to consider whether there was any real reason to be frightened, and introduce the legend that tells of the first 'Christmas tree'.

The Legend of St Boniface

Forests can be frightening places, especially when you are alone and it's getting dark. But Boniface wasn't frightened. He was a Christian who believed that God would keep him safe. Boniface wanted others to trust in God as well. So he journeyed across Germany teaching people about Jesus.

Often his journeys took him through forests. One winter's day the wind shook the branches of the trees so that they looked like long arms reaching out to grab him. Some made eerie creaking noises as they moved. Sometimes there was a sharp crack as two branches hit against each other. It seemed as if the trees were alive!

Boniface shivered and drew his cloak around him. The shadows were getting darker. Soon it would be night. Boniface often travelled the forest by the light of the moon. He had often heard the howling of wolves and the screeching of owls. But suddenly he was startled by a different kind of cry.

Above the noise of the wind he heard a terrified scream, and the sound of voices chanting. Boniface drew back into the shadows as the voices came nearer. A group of hooded figures dragged a struggling boy along the track. They stopped beneath a large tree. The chanting grew louder. They pushed the boy to the ground and Boniface was horrified to see one of the figures raise an axe high in the air. The boy screamed again in terror.

Boniface could stand it no longer. Racing from his hiding place he seized the axe and helped the boy to his feet. The figures surrounded him menacingly. 'You shall die for this,' they hissed. 'The spirits of the trees demand life, and they will now take yours.'

'I am not afraid,' replied Boniface, 'and you should not be frightened of the spirits of the trees. Look! I will show you that they have no power.'

Taking the axe, Boniface began to cut at the trunk of the ancient oak tree that the people worshipped. They drew back, believing he would come to harm. Eventually, the tree crashed to the ground and Boniface stood there wiping his brow and smiling.

Everyone was amazed. 'What is this new magic?' they asked one another.

'It's not magic,' said Boniface. 'It is the strength that comes from faith in God. God, who made the trees, has sent his Son so that we need never be afraid.' As he sat on the upturned tree telling the story of Jesus' birth, Boniface noticed a tiny fir tree growing in the soil around its roots.

He paused and pointed to it. 'Look,' he said. 'If you wish to have a sacred tree, here is one. Its branches point to heaven and to God who has made the world. Its leaves are evergreen and a sign of eternal life. It is the tree of peace for you to make homes from its wood.'

It was now night and the moon was shining. Quietly they gazed at the tiny tree bathed in silvery light. The wind had stopped and everything in the forest was still.

3. Were any aspects of the story frightening? Invite the children to reflect quietly upon times when they have been afraid. Can the children remember and understand the qualities that St Boniface saw in the fir tree? At the centre of our Christmas celebrations is a tree that points us to God and to the peace found by those who trust in him.

4. Point out that many people, including Christians, have rediscovered the value of nature and the way that God speaks to us through the natural world. We wouldn't want to chop down a huge oak tree today, but in the legend it was a way of showing the people that they didn't have to kill a young boy to please the tree.

 ## Time for reflection

Creator God,
Thank you for trees.
Thank you that there are so many different types of tree
and that they provide oxygen for us to breathe,
fuel for us to burn,
homes for many different creatures,

shelter and shade,
and beauty for us to look at and enjoy.

Help us, like St Boniface,
to stand up for what is right
and help us to grow like a strong oak tree,
and to point to you and your love
like a tall, straight Christmas tree.
Amen.

 Song

'O Christmas tree' (*Carol, Gaily Carol*, 41)
'Think of a world' (*Come and Praise*, 17)

THE SHEPHERD'S STORY

By the Revd Guy Donegan-Cross

Suitable for Whole School

Aim

To celebrate the Christmas message in a humorous way.

Preparation and materials

- Shepherd's outfit (dressing gown and tea towel!), animal figurine, simple wooden cross, doll in baby clothes.
- This is simply a monologue which you can perform with as much gusto as you can muster. You don't need to stick to the script – the props can act as your guide.

Assembly

(Enter dressed as a shepherd, with your bag over your shoulder.)

You'll never guess where I've just come from. A bloke like me; who'd have thought it? A simple, smelly shepherd! I mean, I have just seen the most amazing thing you could ever hope to see. And what's more, I've got some things in here to prove it (*point to bag*).

It all began the other night. Some of us were all sitting round minding our sheep and washing our socks, when suddenly there was this enormous light in the sky and the sound of singing like you've never heard before. We all looked up with our mouths open like this (*open mouth*).

Suddenly, one of the angels who was there said, 'Oi, you!' At least I think it was something like that but I can't quite remember, we were just sitting down with our mouths open. 'Get down to Bethlehem,' he said. 'The king of the world is about to be born and he wants you to go and see him.'

'All right,' I said. 'But who's going to look after the sheep?'

'Don't worry about that,' said the angel. 'You just get down to Bethlehem and we'll mind your sheep – we're quite good at that.'

So we ran down to Bethlehem, and we found him. It was the most amazing night of my life. The king of the world – a baby! When he saw me, the baby looked at me and laughed – at least I think it was laughing, I'm not very good with baby sounds. His mother Mary was there and she was such a sweetie. In fact, after I had been there a while I asked if I could take a few things just to remind myself of what I had seen. You know, souvenirs and things like that. And she said, 'No problem.'

Would you like to see them? Okay. Well, the first thing I've got is this little cow (take out animal). Okay, I know it's a bit small but I couldn't bring you the real thing, could I? Do you know what this reminds me of? Well, the place they were in was a stable, and it was smelly. I mean soooo smelly. You might expect a king to be born in a palace, but this one was born in straw and in the most cramped little place. But it was still wonderful, and in a funny kind of way it seemed right.

I'll show you the next thing, then. I asked Mary if I could take a bit of wood from the stable, just to remind me of the place. She said, 'Fine.' But when I picked this up, she got the strangest look on her face (bring out the cross). I mean, I don't know what all the fuss was about – it's only two bits of wood.

But the best thing I took I've saved till last. You see, we all felt that this was so special, that the baby was a gift. So I thought I had better do something about that (take doll out of the bag). So I've got him here. I figured if he was a gift then I had better take him with me.

Why are you laughing? I haven't done anything wrong have I? But ... Oh, you mean, he's a gift for everyone?

Silly me!

Oh well, I suppose I'd better go and take him back. They'll be wondering where he is. Goodbye, then.

(*Walk off, cuddling and talking to doll.*)

 Time for reflection

Shepherds watched their flocks.
Angels – shepherds shocked!

New-born boy – shepherds joy.
New-born king – angels sing.
Christmas story – glory, glory.

 Song

'Rise up, shepherd' (*Come and Praise*, 116)

EPIPHANY

By the Revd Sue Allen

Suitable for Whole School

 Aim

To explore the meaning of Epiphany: God showing that he cares not just about one group of people, but for everyone.

 Preparation and materials

- You will need some chocolate money or other 'gold', an incense stick and a jar of skin cream, such as Nivea, labelled as 'cream for wrinkly bodies'.
- Prepare a card, OHP or flip-chart with the word Epiphany on it.
- Prepare seven cards with the letters S H O W I N G on them, or write these on a flip-chart or OHP at the appropriate point.

 Assembly

1. As the children come in, they should be able to see the display of 'gold' coins, the incense stick burning, and the jar of cream. Invite them to look at the items and offer suggestions as to what the assembly is about. Go through the visual aids one by one, explaining that the skin cream represents myrrh, which used to be put on the wrinkly skin of dead bodies!

   Include a brief reminder that God's people had been looking for someone to lead them and their nation. (This links well with the Christmas and Advent assemblies also on the site.)

2. Introduce the word 'Epiphany', held up or pointed to by a volunteer. To explore what 'Epiphany' means, tell the story of the coming of the Wise Ones, with the help of seven volunteers, each holding up a letter, as follows:

W – Wise Ones, from a far country
S – the Star, which they followed, looking for a king
H – Herod, the king they found, who was
N – not pleased to hear about a New king!
O – over the place where Jesus was, where the star stopped where they Offered him
G – Gifts, of gold,
I – Incense, and also myrrh.

3. Invite the children to put up their hands when they have worked out what word can be made by rearranging the letters – SHOWING – and move volunteers' positions as required (or rewrite on the flip-chart/OHP).

4. Say that the message of Epiphany is that God is showing himself to ALL people; we are all special to him.

 Time for reflection

Thank God for his care for all of us.
Pray that we may all know he loves us.

S   is for the Star
H   is for Herod
O   is for Offering
W   is for Wise Ones
I   is for Incense
N   is for Naughty Herod not happy with the New king
G   is for Gifts

All together – SHOWING God cares for us all.

 Song

'Oi Oi we are gonna praise the Lord' (*Songs of Fellowship for Kids*; Praise CD)
'Riding out across the desert' (*Come and Praise*, 124)

CARING FOR GOD'S CREATURES

By the Revd Guy Donegan-Cross

Suitable for KS2

 Aim

To explore the idea that animal conservation is part of stewarding God's world.

 Preparation and materials

- *Optional*: A video clip showing animal conservation in action (see 1. below).

 Assembly

1. An excellent way to start is with a video showing issues of conservation. Steve Irwin, the Australian conservationist, is brilliant at leaping onto dangerous animals, being enthusiastic about them, and highlighting issues of conservation. After the video clip, say that conservationists like Steve Irwin often say that people are more dangerous to animals than animals are to people.

2. If you don't have a video clip, you can start here! Say that you are going to read out the names of some creatures. After each name you want the children to guess whether the creature is a bird, an animal or a fish. Read each name and then ask the children to put up their hands to show which option they think it is. Give the answer after each question.

> Cottidae (fish)
> Lord Howe white-eye (bird)
> Salado shiner (fish)
> Flat-headed myotis (animal)
> Black mamo (bird)
> Bagangan (fish)

Cayman hutia (animal)
Thicktail chub (fish)
Lesser Cuban nesophont (animal)
New Caledonia wood rail (bird)
Lesser bilby (animal)
Oahu 'akepa (bird)

3. After the quiz, ask the children what they think all the creatures have in common. Answer: you will not find any of them anywhere on earth. They are all extinct. And some of them are extinct because of the actions of people. Say that we have a job to do – to look after animals, particularly endangered species. Give the example of the Sumatran tigers – there are only 400 left in the wild.

4. Tell the children about St Francis, who lived a long time ago (800 years). He loved animals and had a special relationship with them. He would pick worms up off the road so they would not get trodden on! Tell the following story:

One day, Francis and his friends were walking through the Spoleto valley in Italy. Suddenly, Francis spotted a great number of birds. There were doves, crows, every variety of bird you could think of. Swept up in the moment, Francis left his friends in the road and ran after the birds, who patiently waited for him. He greeted them in his usual way, expecting them to scurry off into the air as he spoke. But they didn't move.

Amazed, he asked them if they would stay for a little while to hear about God. He said to them: 'My brother and sister birds, you should praise your Creator and always love him: he gave you feathers for clothes, wings to fly and all other things that you need. It is God who made you noble among all creatures, making your home in the thin, pure air. Without sowing or reaping, you receive God's guidance and protection.'

At this the birds began to spread their wings, stretch their necks and gaze at Francis, rejoicing and praising God in a wonderful way. Francis then walked through the middle of the flock of birds, touching their heads and bodies with his tunic. Then he gave them his blessing, making the sign of the cross over them. At that they flew off and Francis, rejoicing and giving thanks to God, went on his way.

Later, Francis wondered aloud to his companions why he had never preached to the birds before. And from that day on, Francis made it his habit to tell all birds, animals and reptiles to praise and love the God who made them. And many times during Francis's life there were remarkable events of Francis speaking to the animals. There was even a time when St Francis quieted a flock of noisy birds that were interrupting a church service! Much to the wonder of all present, the birds remained quiet until Francis had finished preaching.

5. Conclude that Francis looked after animals because he believed one thing: that everything in the world belongs to God, and so all animals need looking after, especially the ones that may disappear.

 Time for reflection

Dear God,
Thank you that everything belongs to you.
Help us to care for the creatures you have made.
Amen.

 Song

'God in his love' (*Come and Praise*, 76)

TRUE SUPPORTERS

By the Revd Alan M. Barker

Suitable for KS2

Aim

To explore issues of loyalty and peer-group pressure with reference to the events of Holy Week and the experience of the disciple Peter.

Preparation and materials

- A golf club or alternative item of sports equipment and three easily recognizable football scarves, together with some awareness of how the respective teams are performing! Children will probably be able to supply both scarves and information. (These items should be kept hidden until each is required.)
- Colleague(s) prepared with suitable taunts and jibes for the first part.
- Reader(s) for the Bible reading.
- Note: This assembly is a case of 'know your audience', since the merits and achievements of football teams can produce excitement bordering on riot! The suggested outline below can be adapted to keep things cooler if necessary; you could, for example, cut down on the personal element by cutting out the jibes and being more factual. Or tell it as a story about different teams – perhaps made-up ones or those from another European country or an African league.
- You could also change the main sport from football to tennis or motor racing.

Assembly

1. Bring out the first of the scarves, e.g. Manchester United. Inform the children that you are an enthusiastic supporter ...

believe that Alex Ferguson is the best manager in the premiership ... that there's no better team. Look surprised when a colleague interjects with something like: 'But they're not in the FA Cup any more. They were knocked out by Middlesbrough. Anyway *everybody* supports Manchester United. Get a life!'

2. Throw to one side the first scarf and reveal the second, e.g. Liverpool: Actually, not *everyone* supports Manchester United. I'm planning to get a season ticket for Liverpool. Liverpool supporters are the best in the land. You should be in the crowd when they sing: 'You'll never walk alone ... Walk on ... Walk on.' Look taken aback when a colleague again interjects: '*You* should walk on! You've never been to Liverpool. Have some respect and support a local team!'

3. The scarf should again be thrown to one side. Reveal the third scarf, e.g. of a local team. Of course, you *do* support your local team as well, and you always wear their colours. Football's far bigger than the premiership. It's a matter of local pride. You'd never miss a match. Appear pained when a colleague comments: 'But what a bunch of losers. Who'd ever support a 1st/2nd/3rd division club? What a way to spend a Saturday afternoon. Were you there when they lost to...? They'll never get promotion or even manage to stay in the division!'

4. Throw the scarf to one side and take up a position with the golf club. As I was saying ... I'm very enthusiastic about golf...

5. Invite the children to consider whether they have ever 'changed their colours' because of other people's insults. Have there been occasions when they have 'joined the gang' and been unkind just for the sake of it? Reflect upon the very real pressures that are felt when we wish to be accepted and to fit in with the crowd.

   Refer back to the behaviour demonstrated earlier. Surely a true football supporter would be ashamed of deserting their team. Loyalty matters.

   Explain that loyalty means being true to your beliefs and to your friends. It can mean being a 'supporter' during difficult times, without giving up.

6. Remind the children that the story of Holy Week highlights important issues of loyalty:

On Palm Sunday Jesus rode into Jerusalem on a donkey. He was surrounded by his friends and welcomed by crowds of supporters. They waved palm branches, cheered, and chanted: 'Hosanna! (Hurray!) Welcome to the one who comes in the name of the Lord.'

But only a few days later, on Good Friday, Jesus stood alone before a crowd who shouted: 'Kill him! Kill him!' What had happened?

Jesus had been arrested by his enemies and his friends and supporters had run away.

7. Highlight the experience of the disciple Peter by inviting someone to read from a modern translation of the Bible the story of how he denies Jesus (Luke 22.54–62, GNB version below). This could be arranged as a dramatic reading using a number of voices.

They arrested Jesus and took him away into the house of the High Priest; and Peter followed at a distance. A fire had been lit in the centre of the courtyard, and Peter joined those who were sitting round it. When one of the servant women saw him sitting there at the fire, she looked straight at him and said, 'This man too was with Jesus!'

But Peter denied it, 'Woman, I don't even know him!'

After a little while a man noticed Peter and said, 'You are one of them, too!'

But Peter answered, 'Man, I am not!'

And about an hour later another man insisted strongly, 'There isn't any doubt that this man was with Jesus, because he also is a Galilean!'

But Peter answered, 'Man, I don't know what you are talking about!'

At once, while he was still speaking, a cock crowed. The Lord turned round and looked straight at Peter, and Peter remembered that the Lord had said to him, 'Before the cock crows tonight, you will say three times that you do not know me.' Peter went out and wept bitterly.

Peter had discovered how difficult it is to be a true supporter. But, Jesus did not give up supporting Peter. After Easter Day, Jesus asked him to help care for others. Then, Peter's tears were turned to happiness. He had learned from his mistakes.

Loyalty mattered in the friendship between Peter and Jesus. And it continues to be vital within faith and friendship, whichever football team we follow!

 Time for reflection

Lord God, help us to be loyal friends.
We are sorry that sometimes we say one thing and do another.
Thank you that you promise to help and support us, today and always.
Amen.

 Song

'I have decided to follow Jesus' (*Junior Praise*, 98)
'At the name of Jesus' (*Come and Praise*, 58)

MARY'S STORY

By Gill Hartley

Suitable for Whole School

Aim

To consider the story of Jesus' resurrection from the perspective of Mary Magdalene. To reflect on her joy and amazement that Jesus was alive again!

Preparation and materials

- A copy of the script for each performer.
- A Bible in a modern translation or a children's version.
- Prepare the play in advance with six (or seven) older children – you can either read the part of the narrator yourself, or give it to a strong reader.

Assembly

1. Start with the song: 'From the darkness came light' (*Come and Praise*, 29).
2. Read the story of Mary's visit to Jesus' tomb (John 20.1–18) in a modern translation or from a children's version of the Bible.
3. Perform the dramatized reading.

Mary's Story
(based on Luke 24.1–3, John 20.1–18)

Cast: Mary Magdalene, Two Angels, Peter, John, Jesus, Narrator.

Narrator Jesus is dead. Mary and some of her friends get up early on the Sunday morning to go to his tomb with the spices and perfumes they have prepared for his body. When they get there they discover that the stone which had covered the way in has been rolled to one side and the body is gone. Mary runs back to tell Peter and John what has happened.

Mary   (*out of breath*) They've taken Jesus out of his tomb and we don't know where they've put him!

Peter   (*to John, surprised*) We'd better go and have a look!

Narrator Peter and John arrive at the tomb with Mary following behind.

Peter   (*amazed*) The body's gone!

John   (*even more amazed*) You're right! I don't understand.

Narrator Later, Mary stands by herself by the tomb, crying. Then she looks in and sees two angels.

Angels   Why are you crying?

Mary   They've taken Jesus away and I don't know where they've put him!

Narrator Mary turns round and sees Jesus but does not recognize him. She thinks he is the gardener.

Mary   If you've moved him, Sir, tell me where you've put him and I'll take him away.

Jesus   Mary!

Mary   (*amazed*) Jesus?

Jesus   Don't touch me yet, but go back to my brothers and tell them I am not dead.

Narrator Mary runs back to tell Peter and John what has happened.

Mary   (*overjoyed*) I've seen the Lord! He's told me to tell you that he's not dead!

4. Thank the performers and ask them to return to their places.
5. Ask the children how they think the people in the story felt, e.g. Mary: sad at first, then puzzled, then amazed, then overjoyed. Peter and John: surprised, amazed, sure Jesus was God's Special One.
6. Ask the children, why was everyone amazed? Try to bring out the wonder of the fact that someone they had seen die had now been seen alive!

Time for reflection

Dear God,
Thank you for all that amazes us and gives us joy:
that from the darkness comes light,
that after the dead of winter comes the new life of spring,
that out of the egg comes a baby bird,
from a tiny seed comes a tall tree or beautiful flower
and from a dry chrysalis comes a brilliant butterfly.

As Jesus' first followers were amazed and happy at his
   resurrection,
help us never to lose our amazement at the wonder of new life
   all around us.
Amen.

 ## Song

'From the darkness came light' (*Come and Praise*, 29)

Stories from the Bible

THE SIXTH WORD

By Gordon and Ronni Lamont

Suitable for Whole School

Note: The title comes from the word 'created' – it's the sixth word in the Good News Bible. If your version is different, rename the assembly accordingly!

Aim

To celebrate creativity and the fact that God has made us to create together.

Preparation and materials

● You may find it useful to have a Bible to hand.

Assembly

1. Ask if anyone knows who the first person in the Bible is. You might get God, Adam or Eve. Explain that they're all wrong – it's Chap One! Omit this 'joke' if it's too terrible to use.

   Explain that you're going to read from the very beginning of the Bible. If appropriate, describe the Bible and the Old Testament briefly, pointing out that it's a special book for Jews, Christians and Muslims.

   Read Genesis 1.1 and ask the children to listen carefully. Say that there are some very important words in this tiny half-sentence. 'In the beginning, when God created the universe'.

2. Split the assembly into groups (eight would be right for the Good News Bible version), and give each group one word from the reading:

   In
   the
   beginning,
   when
   God

created
the
universe

Then play with the words – you conduct the different groups to say their word in turn. Start by putting them all in order, then jumble them up, ending with overlapping words. You'll need to set some group rules for this in advance – the children should watch you carefully, and you'll indicate by conducting who is to speak and at what volume.

Play around with this for a while to produce a choral poem based on the words.

3. Explain that you've just made a choral poem together. Everyone's been involved in creating it. Point out that right at the beginning of the Bible, God created things. It's the first thing God did – it doesn't say: 'In the beginning God woke up and made a cup of tea', or 'In the beginning God did a SATS test', or 'In the beginning God watched telly'.

According to the Bible, the first thing God did was make something, create something – in fact it was the universe, so there was probably a need to watch a bit of telly afterwards...

4. Ask the children if they will be Godlike today – what will they create?

Time for reflection

Dear God,
In the beginning you created things.
Thank you that you made us to create things.
Help us all to use our creative talents,
to discover what they are,
to grow them and to develop new talents.
Amen.

Song

'Let's sing and dance' (*Come and Praise Beginning*, 58)

A CAMEL THROUGH THE EYE OF A NEEDLE

By Gill O'Neill

Suitable for KS2

Aim

To illustrate Jesus' saying that it is easier for a camel to pass through the eye of a needle than for a rich person to enter the kingdom of heaven.

Preparation and materials

- You will need three PE hoops of different sizes, and a needle threaded with cotton, preferably out of sight of the children.

Assembly

1. Begin the assembly by asking for two volunteers to come and hold the largest hoop for you. They should hold the hoop so that it is vertical, and about 50 cm from the floor.

   Now ask for a volunteer who thinks they can pass through the hoop. You could choose several different children, starting with a smaller child and ending with someone taller.

   After the last child has climbed through the largest hoop ask them if it was easy. Hopefully they will say yes.

2. Now ask the same child or children if they can do it again. Change the large hoop for the middle-sized hoop, and let them climb through. You could encourage the children in the audience to applaud.

   Again ask the children if that was easy.

3. Change this hoop for the smallest version – you can make a fuss as you hold up the hoop, as if you were a magician's assistant. The audience may be encouraged to gasp!

Ask the children to get through this hoop as best they can. On completion again encourage the audience to clap and ask the children to return to their seats.

Put the hoops down, but keep the two volunteer hoop holders at the front.

4. Next, ask the assembled children if there is anyone who can do a convincing impression of a camel. Choose someone who you think will be confident, and ask them to join you at the front. As the child starts their impression, ask him/her to demonstrate the following to the audience:

Camels have big eyes,
and long fluttery eyelashes,
four legs,
and a hump.

5. Ask the first two volunteers to hold up the largest hoop again. Now ask the 'camel' to climb through each hoop in turn (preferably in character). The smallest hoop may cause difficulties.
6. Finally take out your needle and hold it up to the audience. Slowly pull out the strand of cotton, and attempt to look through the eye.

Explain to the 'camel' that as it is so clever, perhaps it could try to go through the eye of the needle. Your two volunteers could hold the needle low for the camel to climb over, and up high for the camel to go under; 'The camel can go over it. It can go under it. But no, it can't go through it!' (Many of the children may recognize this line as being similar to 'Going on a Bear Hunt'.)
7. Now read Luke 18.18–27 from a children's Bible (or use the Good News Bible version below).

A Jewish leader asked Jesus, 'Good Teacher, what must I do to receive eternal life?'

'Why do you call me good?' Jesus asked him. 'No one is good except God alone. You know the commandments: Do not commit adultery; do not commit murder; do not steal; do not accuse anyone falsely; respect your father and your mother.'

The man replied, 'Ever since I was young, I have obeyed all these commandments.'

When Jesus heard this, he said to him, 'There is still one more thing you need to do. Sell all you have and give the money to the poor, and you will have riches in heaven; then come to me and follow me.' But when the man heard this, he became very sad, because he was very rich.

Jesus saw that he was sad and said, 'How hard it is for rich people to enter the Kingdom of God! It is much harder for a rich person to enter the Kingdom of God than for a camel to go through the eye of a needle.'

The people who heard him asked, 'Who, then, can be saved?'

Jesus answered, 'What is impossible for man is possible for God.'

Conclude that what often happens is that people get so caught up with the things they own, and in striving for more things, that they forget what is truly important about being a good person.

8. You could also point out that some people who study the Bible think that Jesus was talking about a gate in the Jerusalem city wall, which was small and called 'the eye of the needle'. Rich people and their camels would only fit through if they took all their valuable possessions off the camel first.

 Time for reflection

You could light a candle for the children to focus on. Ask the children to think about the following:

Think of a time when you were so pleased with the things you have, perhaps birthday presents, sweets or pocket money, but forgot to share.

Think of a time when you were so busy thinking about winning a game, you didn't notice someone hurting.

Think about a time when you were so busy with lots of friends, you didn't notice someone feeling lonely.

Help us, Lord, to think of others, not only ourselves.
May we offer our help and friendship, and learn to share with others.

Help us to see that by sharing and caring we make not only others,
but also ourselves, feel so much happier.
Amen.

 Song

'Thank you Lord for this new day' (*Come and Praise*, 32)

NOAH AND HIS ARK

By the Revd Alan M. Barker

Suitable for KS1/Whole School

Note: Although it can stand alone, this assembly is Part 1 of a three-part series on Noah.

Aim

To retell part of the story of Noah and to reflect upon the need to protect endangered animal species.

Preparation and materials

- You will need a picture of a giant panda.
- Devise a list of familiar animals and birds, together with some brief descriptions for use in the story.
- Have available some chairs or blocks to create a pretend 'ark'.
- For further information and pictures, go to www.panda.org (the WWF website).

Assembly

1. Begin by saying that some of the stories found in the Bible are many thousands of years old. They have been passed down from one generation to another. They are important stories because they can help us to understand how to live in God's way, caring for one another, and for all the earth's creatures.

2. Introduce the story of Noah's Ark. Explain that the word ark means 'boat'. Invite the children to take part in the story by identifying different creatures from the descriptions that you will give: e.g. I have whiskers. I can move very quietly to catch mice and birds. I purr when I am happy. I enjoy drinking milk and could live in your house. I am a cat.

3. Noah's Ark
Based on Genesis 6.5–22

(During the story, fill up a pretend ark with children playing Noah's sons and representing pairs of different creatures.)

Noah felt sad. He was unhappy because the earth had been spoiled. People were fighting and quarrelling with one another. The beautiful forests had been burned and the animals were afraid. There was no peace for any creature.

Noah was a good man and he felt that God must be sad too. 'What can we do?' he prayed. 'We must start again', said God. 'Build a boat for yourself. Build a big one with room for yourself and your family. Make sure you build it well, because I'm going to make it rain. The whole world will be covered with water. And don't forget the animals and birds. Make room in your boat for them as well.'

Noah built his ark with the help of his sons: Shem, Ham and Japheth. (Invite three children to help construct a simple 'ark' by making a circle of chairs with an opening on one side.) Eventually he and his family were able to make it their home.

'We mustn't forget the animals and birds,' said Noah. Together they thought about all the creatures that needed to be brought into the boat.

They thought about tiny creatures, with long tails, that scurried about and squeaked, and sometimes ate their cheese. *(Invite the child who recognizes that these are mice on board the ark – and ask them to bring a friend.)*

They thought about big creatures with strong backs and manes and tails of flowing hair. How would they get them in? *(Invite the child who recognizes horses into the ark – and ask them to bring a friend.)*

They thought of the big brown birds that laid the eggs that Noah and his family ate for breakfast (*hens*).

And they couldn't ignore the animal that dropped its bone and started barking loudly, wagging its tail (*dog*).

(Describe some other creatures, or ask the children to do so, in order for others to guess their identity.)

Eventually every kind of creature went into Noah's boat. They knew that they would be safe and looked after. A week later, it began to rain and rain and rain!

4. Say that you are stopping the story there for today, because there are some things you want the children to think about. Reflect that there are many different kinds of animal – far too many to include them all in the story. Do the children keep any animals as pets? How do they care for them?

5. Explain that it's still important for people to care for the earth's creatures, just as Noah did. Show the picture of the giant panda. It's the emblem of the WWF. Pandas live in China, but very few are found in the wild. Human beings are destroying the secret places where they are able to live. Today, there are other places of safety besides the 'ark'. Explain that some pandas are kept in zoos where those who care for them are trying to increase the numbers of baby pandas that are born. Others are being protected in panda reserves – areas of forest where there are plenty of the bamboo shoots that they need to eat and where the pandas are protected from hunters.

In conclusion, reflect that although the story of Noah is very old it can help us remember to care for animals, especially those that are in danger today.

 ## Time for reflection

Creator God,
Thank you for the wonderful animals and birds that live with
    us on earth.
Help us to protect them from harm,
and to care for all creatures.
Amen.

 ## Song

Whole School: 'Think of a world without any flowers' (*Come and Praise*, 17)
KS1: 'Mr Noah built an ark', an adaptation of 'Old MacDonald had a farm' (below)

Mr Noah built an ark,
E-I-E-I-O
And in that ark he had some mice

E-I-E-I-O
With a squeak, squeak here (*etc.*)

Have fun with subsequent verses including elephants, hens, and dogs, etc. Concluding verse:

Mr Noah built an ark
E-I-E-I-O
And soon the rain began to fall
E-I-E-I-O
With a splish splash here
and a splish splash there
Here a splish, there a splash,
Everywhere a splish, splash.
Mr Noah built an ark
E-I-E-I-O!

NOAH AND THE FLOOD

By the Revd Alan M. Barker

Suitable for KS1/Whole School

Note: Although it can stand alone, this assembly is Part 2 of a three-part series on Noah.

Aim

To retell part of the story of Noah and to reflect upon our experience of rainy weather.

Preparation and materials

- You will need to be familiar with the story to be able to tell it with appropriate actions.
- One child could be prepared to play the part of the dove and will need a leafy twig.
- The rhyme could be displayed on an OHP.

Assembly

1. Ask the children to think of a really rainy day. When did it last rain heavily? Reflect upon the effect that rain has on a day at school. Include reference to journeys to and from school being difficult and wet. What special clothes are worn?

   Is it harder for the drivers of buses and cars to see where they are going? What do the children like/dislike about wet days? How does rain affect outdoor activities and playtimes? Sometimes we have to patiently wait for the rain to stop before going outside.

2. Remind the children of the story of Noah's Ark. Noah was told by God to build a huge boat, or ark, because it was going to rain. Every kind of animal and bird was given a home inside.

   Continue the story, inviting the children to join in the

actions and the counting. If the children are young, the counting can be adapted into four lots of ten (another ten days!). One child might play the part of the dove, being sent on short flights out of the room.

3. **Noah's Ark**
   Based on Genesis 7—8

It rained and rained. (*Imitate rain with fingers.*) Noah and the animals watched as the puddles grew deeper and wider. Soon they became streams of running water. (*Illustrate with appropriate actions.*) It kept on raining. Soon Noah's ark was floating in a vast sea of water. The water was grey. The sky was dark. And inside everyone felt gloomy as well.

Together they counted the days and nights. 1, 2, 3, 4, 5, 6, 7, 8, 9, 10 days and nights (*count off on fingers and hold out hands to feel for rain*). It was still raining!

11, 12, 13, 14, 15, 16, 17, 18, 19, 20 days and nights (*count off on fingers and hold out hands again*). It was still raining!

21, 22, 23, 24, 25, 26, 27, 28, 29, 30 (*count off on fingers and feel for rain*). Would it ever stop?

31, 32, 33, 34, 35, 36, 37, 38, 39. The animals could still hear the rain beating on the roof of the ark (*count off on fingers and drum finger tips*).

40. 'It's stopped!' (*everyone still*).

But it was many more days before a breeze blew and began to dry the water up. And it was many more days still before there was a sudden bump! The ark had hit dry land. Soon the animals would be able to go outside again.

Noah let a dove fly out to see how dry it was. At first the dove came back quickly because there was nowhere to land. A week later the dove brought a fresh twig back in its beak. Noah knew that the water had gone down far enough for the tree tops to grow again. Two weeks later the dove didn't come back. The land was dry again, and the animals got ready to go outside!

4. Refer to any recent coverage of flooding in the news. Explain that lots of heavy rain can cause rivers to overflow, covering roads and damaging homes. Then everyone must wait for the rain to stop and for the flooding to stop – just like Noah did.

5. If older children are present, refer to global warming and

changed weather patterns caused by atmospheric pollution. While heavy rain isn't punishment sent from God, we do know that it can result from destruction of the environment caused by the carelessness of human beings. The story of Noah has a modern parallel.

6. Reflect that we can't ever stop it raining. But we have to make sensible plans for when it does rain. For some towns and villages beside rivers this might mean building walls and barriers to keep flood water away from buildings. For the children it might mean wearing 'wet-weather' clothing going to and from school. At school it involves having activities for wet playtimes. For Noah it meant building a boat!

7. Explore the meaning of the rhyme:

> Whether the weather be fine,
> or whether the weather be not,
> Whether the weather be cold,
> or whether the weather be hot,
> We'll weather the weather,
> whatever the weather,
> Whether we like it or not.

 ## Time for reflection

Read the rhyme again.

> Dear God,
> Thank you for the rain that makes things grow.
> Thank you that there are all types of weather.
> Help us to make the most of it – whatever the weather!
> **Amen.**

 ## Song

'Incy Wincy Spider' – who also had to wait for the rain to stop.

NOAH AND THE RAINBOW

By the Revd Alan M. Barker

Suitable for KS1/Whole School

Note: Although it can stand alone, this can be used as the concluding assembly of the three-part series on Noah.

 Aim

To tell the concluding part of the story of Noah and to appreciate our experience of colour.

 Preparation and materials

- Select a series of seven appropriately coloured objects to place side by side in order to form a 'rainbow'.
- A bright rainbow picture could be painted as a 'Thinking of you' card for someone who is unwell.

 Assembly

1. Invite the children to remember an occasion when they have seen a rainbow. Explain that rainbows are seen when the sun shines through rain. They often appear after a storm.
2. Remind the children of the story of Noah's Ark. Noah was told by God to build a huge boat, or ark. Every kind of animal and bird was given a home in the ark. Then it began to rain for 40 days and nights. Remind the children that at the end of the last instalment of the story it had stopped raining and the land had begun to dry and trees and plants to grow again. Continue the story.
3. **Noah's Ark**
   Based on Genesis 9.1–17

   (*As each colour is mentioned introduce the similarly coloured item, and invite the children to suggest others that might be included.*)

Noah and his family were tired and sad. The animals and birds were tired and sad too. They had been in the ark for a very long time. When at last the door was opened they slowly made their way outside. The sky was still cloudy and dull. Smelly black mud covered everything in sight. Everyone was unhappy at what they saw.

But God hadn't forgotten Noah and all the creatures. To make them feel better, he decided to put a rainbow into the cloudy sky. 'I shall make a rainbow,' God said, 'and it will be one of the most beautiful sights in the world.'

So, first of all, God made a stripe of red. 'In my new world,' he said, 'red will be the colour of bright poppy flowers, ripe apples and robin's chests.' (*Display the red object and invite the children to think of red things.*)

Then came orange. God said: 'Orange will be the colour of pumpkins, autumn leaves and ginger cats watching goldfish!' (*Invite the children to think of other things that are orange.*)

Yellow was next. God decided that yellow would be the colour of buttercups and the honey made by busy bees. 'And I will hide yellow inside hen's eggs,' he said!'

Here's a nice colour,' God thought, as he mixed green. 'I shall make lots of things that are green, like cabbages and caterpillars, grass, and grasshoppers too.' (*You only have to look around to see that green is one of God's favourite colours.*)

And next to green God put blue and indigo. 'Blue and indigo will be the colour of the sea and the sky,' he decided.

Finally God added purple. 'Purple,' he said, 'will be a very special colour. I will use it for butterfly flowers and hills covered with heather. It will be the colour of delicious grapes and juicy plums.'

Red, orange, yellow, green, blue, indigo and purple all shone brightly together in the rainbow. Noah smiled when he saw the colours in the sky, and the animals felt happy too! It was God's promise that the world would soon be new again.

4. Refer to the objects and point out that they are arranged like a rainbow. Reflect that colours make our world a brighter and happier place. What are the children's favourite colours?

5. If a card has been made, invite those involved to show it to the assembly. Who will it be sent to? Has anyone ever painted

a bright and colourful picture to make somebody feel better?
The rainbow helped Noah to know that God cared. Colourful
cards and flowers can cheer us up when we don't feel very
well or if we feel sad.

 Time for reflection

Lord God,
Thank you for all the colours of the rainbow
which brighten up our homes and school.
Thank you for crayons and paints which are fun to use.
Help us to make the world a happier place for everyone,
especially for those who need our friendship and our care.
Amen.

 Song

'Who put the colours in the rainbow?' (*Come and Praise*, 12)

ACTIONS SPEAK LOUDER THAN WORDS

By the Revd Nicky Carnall

Suitable for Whole School

Aim

To explore the story and its theme of doing good rather than just talking about it.

Preparation and materials

• Practise telling the story (based on Luke 5.17–26) in advance.

Assembly

1. Ask three children to come out to the front to mime certain things, while the other children guess what they are doing, e.g. cleaning windows, driving a car, playing football.
   Make the point that you can tell what somebody's doing just by watching – actions sometimes speak louder than words.
2. Explain that you're going to tell a Bible story about some friends whose actions helped another friend. Say that you will need help with the actions as you go through, and rehearse the following with everyone joining in:

   Fed up (head in hands – 'huh')
   Walk (pat hands on legs to make walking sound)
   Bed (hands together beside head as if asleep, snoring sound)

   Say that every time you mention the key words (in bold), everyone has to join in with the action.
3. Tell the story.

   George was **fed up**. The Bible doesn't say he was called George – that's what I'm calling him. But he was definitely **fed up**.

You see, all his life he'd been able to **walk** about like anyone else. And not only to **walk** – he'd been able to run and jump, to climb steps, and to hop on one leg.

But over the last few months it had all been getting a bit more difficult. It wasn't that George was old – it was just that his legs didn't work as well as they used to. In fact, it had got so bad that George couldn't **walk** at all any more. All he could do was to lie on his **bed**.

You see, in those days – 2,000 years ago – there were no wheelchairs to get your friends to push you about in, or to have races in.

There was no easy way of getting about if your legs didn't work very well and you couldn't **walk**.

So George had to stay at home – lying on his **bed**. And he got more and more **fed up**.

George's friends – Len, Glen, Sven and Monica – would go round to see him. They would tell him jokes to try and cheer him up. And it worked for a while, but then he remembered he couldn't go out so he'd get **fed up** again.

His friends would tell him stories about all the things they had been doing. And that cheered him up for a while, but then he thought about all the things he couldn't do, so he got **fed up** again.

They would tell him about all the people who sent their love and hoped he would get better. And this cheered him up for a bit, but then he realized how much he missed seeing everybody, so he felt **fed up** all over again.

George's friends were at their wit's end. How on earth could they help their friend, who couldn't **walk**, who was always **fed up**, and who just lay there on his **bed**?

Well, one day there was great excitement in the air. People had heard that Jesus was nearby – in a town not far away from where George and his friends lived.

And the thing that everybody knew about Jesus was that he was doing some special and wonderful things. Not only did he tell some really exciting stories, he also made ill people better.

George's friends – Len, Glen, Sven and Monica – met together to talk. They were really excited.

'We need to get Jesus and George together. That way Jesus will make George's legs better – then George will be able to

walk again; he'll be able to get out of **bed**; and he won't be so **fed up**.'

But there was a problem. Jesus was in the next town. How were they going to get George there when he couldn't **walk**? There were no cars or buses in those days.

Suddenly they realized what they had to do. Shouting with excitement, they jumped up and ran to George's house. Without stopping to explain what they were doing, they went to the four corners of George's **bed**, and they lifted it up – with George still lying in the middle of it.

They carried George and his **bed** all the way to the next town. It was a long way and their arms got very tired. And George wasn't very grateful – he kept moaning at them because he was getting terribly jiggled around on his **bed**.

When George and his friends arrived in the next town, they were horrified to discover that the house Jesus was in was already completely full of people. There was no way even one of them could have got in – and there was certainly no way they could have carried a whole **bed** in, with a very **fed up** George on top.

But the friends soon had another idea. They climbed up some steps at the side of the house – all the way up on to the roof. It was a long way up, and it was especially difficult carrying George and his **bed** up there.

But eventually they did it. In just a few minutes the friends had made a hole in the roof – and then, with the help of some strong ropes, they lowered George on his **bed** all the way down, until he landed gently on the floor, just in front of where Jesus was sitting!

Well, you can imagine how surprised Jesus and all the other people in the house were! But Jesus was not shocked for very long. He looked very thoughtfully at George. Without needing to be told, Jesus understood about George no longer being able to **walk**, about him having to stay inside on his **bed**, and about him feeling sad and **fed up**.

Jesus suddenly smiled at George and said, 'Everything you've ever done wrong – it's all been forgiven!'

Everyone in the house started mumbling and muttering to each other. Only God was able to forgive people. What was

Jesus doing, saying that George was forgiven? They didn't realize at that time that Jesus *was* God!

But George understood. He smiled back at Jesus. All of a sudden he didn't feel **fed up** any more. It was like a huge weight had been lifted. It was like all those months of feeling angry and sad and **fed up** were all behind him. He could get on with his life happily again.

And then Jesus said to him, 'George, get up. Pick up your **bed** and **walk!**' And, to the crowd's amazement, George smiled a big broad grin – and he got up! He stood up! And then he started to **walk** around the room! He could hardly believe it.

Before people really understood what was happening, George was hopping and jumping and dancing around the room.

Later on, after George and his friends had said 'thank you' to Jesus, they were all able to **walk** home, dragging the **bed** along behind them. And George said a big 'thank you' to his friends. After all, it was their friendship and their care that had helped him during the months when he couldn't **walk**, and had to stay in **bed**, feeling **fed up**.

And it was their friendship that had taken him to see Jesus – the one who could both forgive people, and help people to **walk** again.

 Time for reflection

George's friends showed by their actions that they cared about him. Not only by taking him to Jesus, but also by going round to see him even when he was sad and fed up.

Also, Jesus told George that he was forgiven and George believed him. But Jesus backed this up with action, by helping to make George better.

For all of us, it's not enough just to say nice things to people – we need to back it up by doing kind and caring things for them too.

Lord Jesus,
We thank you for good friends who care about us
and show their care by their actions.

Help us to be friends to others and to show our care by what
we do.
Amen.

 Song

'When Jesus walked' (*Come and Praise*, 25)
'Hallelu, hallelu' (*Junior Praise*, 67)

PEACE

By Ronni Lamont

Suitable for KS1 and Whole School

 Aim

To explore the idea of peace in our lives.

 Preparation and materials

- Familiarize yourself with the story (based on Mark 4.35–41) and 'join-in' sounds.

 Assembly

1. Tell the children that you are going to tell a story and that you need their help. Practise the following sounds, explaining that they are to join in with the sound when they hear the key words.

   > Lake: **Splash, splash**
   > Sleep/Asleep/Slept: **Snore, snore**
   > Wind: **Ooooo**
   > Waves: **Crash! Crash!**
   > Frightened: **Aaah!**
   > Drown: **Glug**

2. Tell the following story, allowing time for the join-in sounds:

   One day, Jesus and his disciples, his special friends, were down by the **lake**. Jesus was teaching them. Lots of people had come to hear Jesus speaking, and they began to press harder and harder, crowding round Jesus, so he stepped into a boat, and taught them from the side of the **lake**.

   When evening came, the disciples realized that they and Jesus needed to cross the **lake**, to get to the other side. The

lake was very big; in fact it was known as the Sea of Galilee. Jesus was very tired, so as they set off, he settled down in the back of the boat, and went to **sleep**.

The **wind** began to get up as they got out onto the **lake**. The **waves** began to get rougher as they got out onto the **lake**.

The **wind** got stronger and stronger. The **waves** got rougher and rougher. The disciples got more and more **frightened**.

But Jesus **slept** on.

The **wind** got stronger and stronger. The **waves** got rougher and rougher. The disciples got more and more **frightened**.

'Help!' They yelled at Jesus. 'We're going to **drown** and you're **asleep!**'

Jesus woke up, rubbed his eyes and smiled at them. Then he stood up.

'Peace, be still,' he said. And it was.

The **wind** stopped. The **waves** grew calm. And they travelled safely to the other side of the **lake**.

 ## Time for reflection

Think about the times when it seems like you're in the middle of a storm; perhaps when there are arguments or when things seem confusing and difficult or when things are frightening. Think of Jesus being there, saying, 'Peace, be still'. Take a moment now to hear those words, and enjoy the peace they bring.

 ## Song

'Peace is flowing' (*Come and Praise*, 144)

THE LOST COIN

By Gill O'Neill

Suitable for Whole School

Aim

To illustrate, through the parable of the lost coin (Luke 15.8–10), that in God's eyes we are all very precious, and of great worth.

Preparation and materials

- You will need a purse and ten 10p coins. Hide one of these coins in the hall before the assembly, so that it can be found with some searching, the other nine go in the purse.
- A children's Bible containing the story of the parable of the lost coin (or retell it yourself, using the Good News Bible version below).

Assembly

1. Begin the assembly by telling the children that you will need a volunteer to come out and help you do a trick with ten coins.

   Ask the volunteer to count out the coins from the purse. When s/he says, 'Nine', look surprised and explain that they can't have counted them properly. Ask for a recount. When the answer is again, 'Nine', ask the child to sit down while you check. Keep looking puzzled, and turn the purse inside out in search of the missing coin.

   Start to check your pockets and mutter that there were definitely ten coins when you came into the hall this morning. Ask if anyone has seen the lost coin. Perhaps you'd dropped it on your way in. Use your judgement to build up the children's belief that you are really concerned about the missing coin.

   Start to look around the front of the hall, and then enlist

the help of one or two of the children, perhaps asking the seated children for suggestions about where the coin could be.

When the coin is found (you may need to hint where it is if this takes too long) overplay your relief that you've got it back. Explain that it would have driven you mad all day if you hadn't found it.

2. Introduce the story that Jesus told about the woman and the lost coin. Either read it from a children's Bible, or retell it yourself from the version below to engage the listeners (referring to yourself looking for the coin). You could get a child to mime the story while you tell it.

> Suppose a woman who has ten silver coins loses one of them – what does she do? She lights a lamp, sweeps her house, and looks carefully everywhere until she finds it. When she finds it, she calls her friends and neighbours together, and says to them, 'I am so happy I found the coin I lost. Let us celebrate!' In the same way, I tell you, the angels of God rejoice over one sinner who repents.

3. Conclude that what Jesus was saying is that people are like the coins. We are all valuable to God, and even though he has lots of us, if one of us gets lost (by not being the kind of people he'd like us to be) he will not give up hope in us. He will search and search for us until we are found.

 Time for reflection

Ask the children to close their eyes.

> Think about a time when you lost something that is important to you. Think about how you may have spent all day looking for it, perhaps getting frustrated, but being determined to find it.
>
> Remember how relieved and happy you were when you eventually found it, perhaps sharing with your friend or family the news that it had been found.
>
> Let us be thankful that when we are lost, or have gone the wrong way, there are people who care enough for us to search and search, or to show us the right things to do.

Thank you, God, that you love us and keep searching for us. **Amen.**

 Song

'Thank you, Lord' (*Come and Praise*, 32)

'FEELY' FINGERS

By the Revd Alan M. Barker

Suitable for KS1, with option for Whole School

Aim

To be thankful for our sense of touch by exploring the story of how Jesus healed ten men.

Preparation and materials

- This assembly may be used when older children are present (see 2. below) and to heighten awareness of World Leprosy Day. It is, however, suitable for other times.
- You will need contrasting items for the children to feel, e.g. foam ball; rigid ball; ice cubes in small plastic bags; luke-warm water in a plastic bottle; some soft silky material; some sandpaper or a plastic scouring pad. These should be hidden from view to begin with.

Assembly

1. Invite a number of children to the front and ask them to close their eyes and feel the unseen items. Encourage them to describe what they can feel. Is it soft or hard? Is it warm or cold? Is it smooth or rough? What are the children holding?

   Let them open their eyes to see. Were some of the things less pleasant to touch?

   Explain that our sense of touch is an important help in many activities, e.g. when we get dressed (doing up buttons), play ball games, and eat our food.

   Can the children suggest other ways in which touch is important?

2. (*For when older children are present.*) Explain that not everyone is able to feel as well as the volunteers. In some

parts of the developing world children and adults suffer from a disease called leprosy. One of the problems caused by leprosy is a loss of feeling in people's fingers, hands, and feet. Imagine not being able to feel anything properly! How could you tell whether something is very cold or very hot? How difficult everyday tasks would become. You might not be able to tell if you had hurt or cut yourself. Assure the children that with modern medicines people can be cured of leprosy. It is hoped that soon the disease will be largely overcome. It is not found in this country, although it used to be, many, many years ago.

3. There are stories in the Bible telling how Jesus cared for people with leprosy. Invite the children to use their fingers to count to ten in a re-telling of a Bible story (based on Luke 17.11–19) which helps us to say thank you for 'feely' fingers and our sense of touch.

One, two, three, four, five, six, seven, eight, nine, ten men came to see Jesus. 'Can you help us?' they asked. 'No one else will. We can't feel anything.'

One, two, three, four ... ten men held up their fingers. Some were red and sore. There were no friends or family to help put on ointment to make the fingers feel better. Nobody would touch the sore skin, in case they caught it.

But Jesus said, 'You will get better.' He told them to go on their way.

So one, two, three, four ... ten men went on their way, just as he had told them to. They hadn't gone very far when their fingers began to tingle, and then they knew that they were healed.

As they washed their hands they could feel the cool water. They could feel the warmth of the sun. They could feel the smooth skin on their palms and the roughness of their clothes.

One (*raise a single thumb*) man was so pleased and happy that he went back to thank Jesus.

Jesus asked, 'Weren't one, two, three, four ... ten men healed? Where are the other one, two, three, four ... nine? Is it only this one (*single thumb*) who has come back to say thank you?'

Time for reflection

Ask the children to close their eyes and touch their faces with their fingers.

Lord God,
We want to thank you for 'feely' fingers,
for catching things in games,
for warm hands in gloves on cold days,
for cool water in the sea on hot days,
for the wonderful sense of touch.
Amen.

 Song

'It's a new day' (*Come and Praise*, 106)

THE UNFORGIVING SERVANT

By Gordon and Ronni Lamont

Suitable for Whole School

Aim

To think about the parable of the unforgiving servant (Matthew 18.23–35).

Preparation and materials

- Read through the story in advance.

Assembly

1. Explain that today you're going to tell a story that Jesus told about 2,000 years ago. The children have two jobs: one is to join in with the story and the other is to listen carefully and think about it. Explain that the story is a parable – a story with a special meaning.

2. Teach the responses. Whenever you say the word 'king', the children are to say, **Great and powerful one**, and to shape their hands as if putting a crown on their heads.

   Whenever you say the word 'servant', the children are to say, **Your humble servant**, and make a bowing action as they sit.

   Whenever you say the word 'money', the children are to say, **Money, money, money**, and the action is to count out coins in the hand.

   Whenever you say the word 'debt' (you might need to explain this word), the children are to say **Oh dear** and wag their finger in time with the words.

   Practise a few times and then tell the story.

3. Once there was a king
   Great and powerful one

Who had a servant
Your humble servant
And this servant
Your humble servant
Owed the king
Great and powerful one
A lot of money
Money, money, money
A great, great deal of money
Money, money, money
Did the servant
Your humble servant
Owe the king
Great and powerful one

The trouble was that the servant
Your humble servant
Couldn't pay his debt
Oh dear
So, said the king
Great and powerful one
He must go to prison

The servant
Your humble servant
Was brought before the king
Great and powerful one
Please have mercy on me, he said
And he fell on his knees and begged the king
Great and powerful one
And the king
Great and powerful one
Felt sorry for the servant
Your humble servant
And forgave him and let him go

Now the servant
Your humble servant
Went straight out and met a fellow servant
Your humble servant
And this other servant

Your humble servant
Was in debt
Oh dear
To the first servant
Your humble servant
For just a few pounds
Not much money
Money, money, money
At all
It was a very small debt
Oh dear

Pay back the money
Money, money, money
That you owe me
Said the first servant
Your humble servant
The one who the king
Great and powerful one
Had forgiven

The other servant
Your humble servant
Begged to be forgiven his debt
Oh dear
But the first servant
Your humble servant
Would not forgive him and had him thrown in jail

The king
Great and powerful one
Got to hear about the other servant
Your humble servant
Who owed money
Money, money, money
Who was in debt
Oh dear
To the first servant
Your humble servant
Whose debt
Oh dear

The king
Great and powerful one
Had forgiven

He was angry
Very angry
Very, very, very angry
And he sent the first servant
Your humble servant
Straight to prison because that servant
Your humble servant
Had had his debt
Oh dear
Forgiven
But would not forgive a much smaller debt
Oh dear

Time for reflection

Dear God,
Jesus told his followers that they must learn to forgive from
  the heart.
Forgiveness is hard.
When people hurt us we want to hurt them back.
Help us to understand forgiveness,
help us to learn to forgive.
Help us to practise forgiveness whenever we can.
Amen.

Song

'Our Father' (*Come and Praise*, 51)

Festivals of World Religions

By Caroline Donne

As the timing for some of these festivals varies from year to year, we include in these assemblies only the months in which they usually occur. A reliable source of information on the specific dates is the Shap Calendar of Religious Festivals, available from the Shap Working Party, RE Centre, Church House, Great Smith Street, London SW1P 3NZ.

GANESH-CHATURTHI

Hindu festival: August/September

Suitable for Whole School

Aim

To learn about the festival, which celebrates the birth of Ganesh, the elephant-headed god. To focus on the festival's central themes of celebration, new beginnings, and overcoming difficulties.

Preparation and materials

Background
- Be aware that children will have varying depths of knowledge of this story since the celebration of this festival and accounts of the story of Ganesh vary in different parts of India and among Hindu communities around the world. The story adapted for this assembly draws on one of the mainstream versions of the story, but children may be familiar with different versions. If there are Hindu children in the school you could invite them or one of their family to speak about the festival, or to lend you any images or pictures they have of Ganesh.
- The festival lasts for about 7–10 days.

Materials
- A picture of an elephant, a picture of Ganesh. (Useful resources: D. Chatterjee, *The Elephant-Headed God*, Lutterworth Press, 1989; R. Jackson and E. Nesbitt, *Hindu Children in Britain*, Trentham, 1993; Shap Working Party, *Festivals in World Religions*, RMEP, 1998; www.hindunet.org).

Assembly

1. Ask the children if they have ever seen an elephant. What was their reaction? What do people say about elephants? e.g. they

are wise, they are strong, they are gentle, they are good at helping humans, and moving things, they have good memories. Think of other elephants in storybooks, such as Baba or Elma the Patchwork Elephant.

2. Point out that for many millions of Hindus who live in India and around the world, the elephant is one of the most special creatures. This is because one of the most popular Hindu gods is depicted as having the head of an elephant and the body of a man. His name is Ganesh and his birth is celebrated at the time of this festival.

   Go on to say that Hindus worship many gods and goddesses, but they believe that they are all aspects of one god: just like you're one person, but you have many different characteristics (perhaps you're kind, make people laugh and you're brave). Ganesh, the elephant-headed god, has all those aspects that we mentioned to do with elephants at the beginning: he is wise, he is strong, he is gentle, he is kind, he can help with difficult problems.

3. Tell the following story, using the form below or in your own words.

   How did Ganesh get his elephant head? He didn't always have it. The story goes rather like this.

   Ganesh's mother was the goddess Parvati and his father was the god Shiva. One day, not long before Ganesh was born, his father Shiva went on a journey, leaving Parvati at home. Shiva was away for many years, and during that time Ganesh grew from a baby to a young man.

   One spring morning Ganesh was outside when he saw a stranger with long, matted hair, wearing animal skin and with snakes wriggling about him. The stranger wanted to come into the house! He looked frightening and dangerous. Ganesh stood in front of him and tried to stop him because he wanted to protect his mother. What Ganesh didn't know was that this stranger was his father Shiva, and Shiva didn't know that the boy was his son Ganesh. Shiva is known as a quick-tempered god, and he didn't like anyone standing in his way. So he took his sword and cut off the head of Ganesh!

   At that moment Parvati came out, to see her husband with his sword in his hand and her son lying on the ground. 'What have you done, what have you done?' she cried. 'You have killed our son.' Shiva was truly sorry and promised to make things right again, by replacing Ganesh's head with the head of the first living creature he saw.

He searched for many miles. What animal do you think he saw? The first creature he saw was a baby elephant. And that's why Ganesh has the head of an elephant and the body of a man. He has a rather chubby body too, because he is said to like eating sweet things.

4. Explain that at this time of year Hindus celebrate the birth of Ganesh. In many places they make special images of Ganesh and pray to them. They offer him sweet puddings because they know he likes sweet things. They let off fireworks. They make huge images of him and take them on processions.

5. Another thing Ganesh is known for is his beautiful hand-writing and good spelling. If you see a picture of him, you will see that he is holding one of his own tusks, dipped in ink, in one hand and a scroll of paper in the other. It is said that one of the longest poems in the world, telling one of the most important stories for Hindus (the Mahabharata), was dictated to Ganesh, and that he used the pointed end of his tusk dipped in ink to write down the words.

6. Most importantly, Hindus pray to Ganesh before they start anything new, like getting married, moving house, starting a journey, or taking an exam. His image is sometimes placed where new houses are to be built. Hindus believe Ganesh is 'the remover of obstacles': he helps with problems or difficulties that get in the way.

Focus on the themes

Hindus pray to Ganesh because they believe he is wise and he helps at the beginning of new projects or when they start new things.

Talk about the new things that might be happening in the lives of the children or the school.

What words could you use to describe what it feels like to start something new? e.g. scared, excited, not sure what will happen.

What helps you when you have to do something new? e.g.

talking to a friend or someone in your family, thinking carefully about what you will do, asking for God to help.

 ## Time for reflection

Sometimes starting something new feels frightening.
Sometimes starting something new feels exciting.
Sometimes it's difficult to start something new
because there are so many things in the way:
reasons why we shouldn't start, people who try to stop us,
    things we'd rather do.
God of new beginnings, please help us with the new things we
    do today.
Amen.

HOLI

Hindu spring festival: February/March

Suitable for Whole School or Class Assembly

 Themes

The coming of Spring and new life; good is stronger than evil.

 Preparation and materials

Background

- Holi is the Hindu spring festival. Some of the common features are the harvesting of winter crops, and building a bonfire on which coconuts and grain are roasted and shared as *prasada* (holy food). Often young children and babies are carried around the bonfire and this is thought to offer them protection from harm. The image of fire is linked to the story of Prahlada and Holika (see below).
- Sometimes the celebrations are deliberately riotous, for example the squirting of coloured dyes or paints. This is linked with the themes of spring and fertility and can also be traced back to the god Krishna, who liked to play practical jokes and had coloured dye thrown over him by a milkmaid. Very often at Holi people will play practical jokes on one another. It's a festival of great variety and great fun.

Materials

- A picture of flames or a bonfire. Grains of wheat or barley, and fresh coconut. These can be shared out during the assembly, in which case the grains could be lightly baked in oil and honey and the fresh coconut grated or cut into small chunks.
- You will also need a candle.

Assembly

1. Introduce the theme of spring. Talk about the things associated with the coming of spring (e.g. buds on trees, spring flowers, crops beginning to grow, lambs, lighter evenings). Ask the children what they notice about spring and what they like about it. How do things change in the spring? Talk about the differences they notice in the local park, on the journey to school, etc.

2. Hindus, who live in many parts of the world and especially in India, celebrate a spring festival called Holi at this time. It's a time to harvest crops grown in the winter and to give thanks for the coming of the spring.

   At Holi big bonfires are built and lit at night. Ask the children to think about what they like about bonfires. Ask them how they feel when they see the flames leaping in the dark. At the festival of Holi bonfires remind people that the winter days are coming to an end.

   It's a time of hope and a time to celebrate new life. Very often children and babies are carried around the bonfires, because Hindus believe this will keep them safe from harm. Grains are roasted on the fires, and also coconut, and then this food is shared as a way of celebrating Holi and of giving thanks to God (if appropriate you might like to share the coconut pieces and grains with the children at this point).

3. Introduce the story by explaining that there is another link with fire in one of the stories that is often told at Holi. It's the story of the demon Holika and her nephew Prince Prahlada.

   Once there was a cruel and wicked king, who thought that he was so important, that all his people should worship him, just as if he were a god. The king had a son called Prahlada. Prahlada worshipped one of the most important Hindu gods, called Vishnu. He knew that his own father was not a god and that it was wrong to worship him.

   When Prahlada refused to worship his father, the king became furious and he had his own son thrown into a pit full of hissing snakes. But the god Vishnu protected Prahlada and he came out of the snake-pit without a bite.

   Then the king grew even more furious and ordered his son

to be trampled on by a herd of elephants. But again, Vishnu protected Prahlada and he was unharmed.

The wicked king had a wicked sister called Holika. 'I shall ask her to help me,' he thought. Holika had magical powers, which meant that she could not be burned by fire. Together Holika and her wicked brother the king made a plan. Holika took Prahlada to the top of a huge bonfire, expecting him to be burned up in the fire. But Prahlada prayed to Vishnu and suddenly Holika disappeared into the flames. Her magic powers were destroyed and Prahlada was safe.

And so Prahlada, who put his faith in Vishnu, was saved. Hindus tell this story to help them remember that however bad things are, the force of good is more powerful than the force of evil.

 ## Focus on the themes

Talk about the meaning of the story. Why was Prince Prahlada able to walk safely through the flames? Who helped him? Explore the connection between the celebration of Holi and the lighting of bonfires, and the fire in the story. Think about the coming of spring. Why do people think of it as a hopeful time? For many people it is a sign that life goes on. The darkness of winter, when nothing grows, is always followed by spring, when everything begins to grow again.

 ## Time for reflection

Light the candle and invite the children to keep a time of quiet. Ask them to think about what they like about spring.

God of all,
Thank you for the spring.
Thank you for the colours of spring in the blossom on the trees,
in flowering bulbs,
in the different greens of the grass and leaves.
Thank you for the beautiful world that you have made.
Amen.

DIVALI

Hindu festival of lights: October/November

Suitable for Whole School

 Themes

Light; hope; new beginnings.

 Preparation and materials

Background
- Divali (or Deepavali) means a row or string of lights. It lasts from one to five days and for many Hindus it is the new year festival. Rituals and celebrations vary from region to region but the lighting of Diva lamps (traditionally earthenware bowls filled with oil or butter, called ghee, with cotton wicks) is universal. The lamps symbolize the triumph of good over bad, light over darkness.
- The festival is celebrated by Hindus and Sikhs at a time of the darkest night of the lunar month.
- Two stories are often told: the return of Rama and Sita to Ayodhya after the defeat of the demon Ravana; and the story of Lakshmi (goddess of wealth and prosperity), who traditionally blesses homes in which lamps have been lit to greet her.
- For many Hindus it's the beginning of a new business year and prayers are said for a prosperous new year.

Materials
- A Diva lamp or lamps. These could be made in advance as a classroom activity. Take a lump of plasticine, salt dough or clay. Roll it into a ball and pull it into an oval shape. Use the thumb to make an indentation big enough to hold a night-light. Pinch out one end of the lump to make a lip. Flatten the base so that it will stand alone. Leave the lamp to harden and then decorate it. Place a night-light in each lamp.

- Or use a number of candles on stands which can be clearly seen.
- You could make a pathway of Diva lamps or candles at the front of the classroom/school hall, or down the centre of the school hall.
- You could use children's versions of the Rama and Sita story or the story of Lakshmi.

Assembly

1. Think about the word 'darkness' and places that are dark. Ask for volunteers to list some dark places, e.g. bedrooms at night; under the bed; the streets in the evenings at this time of year; caves; a cinema before the film starts. Think about how you feel in dark places, e.g. scared, alone, excited, sad. Explain that places can be dark but our lives can feel dark too when sad, or frightening, or bad things happen. In the same way, people feel that when good things happen their lives feel brighter, like a light coming on.

   Think about what happens when you turn on a light in a dark place. Think about the words that describe that feeling, e.g. safe, hopeful, cheerful.

2. Explain that at this time of year Hindus all over the world meet together for a special festival that celebrates the belief that good is stronger than bad, and they use light to celebrate this belief. The festival is called Divali, which means a row of lights. In the evenings they light small lamps (called Diva lamps) inside and outside their homes to show that light is stronger than darkness, good is stronger than bad. They send cards and they give presents and sweets to one another. They meet together in the temple to pray and give thanks.

   Explain that for many Hindus it is also the beginning of a new year, so it's a time to think about plans for the months ahead, to make a new start and to be hopeful.

3. Tell one of the Divali stories suggested above. If you tell the story of Rama and Sita, emphasize the point that this is a story of good being stronger than bad because Rama and Sita defeat the wicked demon Ravana.

Time for reflection

If you have lit Diva lamps or candles, dim the electric lights and pull the curtains if you can, to create the effect of the light shining in the darkness.

Suggest to the children that they focus on the Diva lights or candles and use the following words to help them to think or to pray about what they have heard.

Light shining in the darkness.
Light takes away the darkness.
Light brings hope.

God of light, when things seem difficult or when we're frightened or sad,
help us to remember that light is stronger than darkness,
good is stronger than bad.

THE PROPHET'S NIGHT JOURNEY AND ASCENSION

Muslim festival

Suitable for Whole School

Aim

To learn why Muslims pray five times a day. To focus on prayer and reflection.

Preparation and materials

Background
- The date of this festival varies according to the lunar calendar.
- There are only two Muslim festivals that are celebrated as an act of religious duty (i.e. they are part of the Five Pillars of Islam). They are the breaking of the fast of Ramadan (Eid-ul-Fitr) and the festival of sacrifice (Eid-ul-Adha) at the end of Hajj (the pilgrimage to Makkah). The Prophet's Night Journey and Ascension is celebrated because it was during this time that the command to pray five times a day (another of the Five Pillars of Islam) was given. It is celebrated by the reading of the Qur'an and extra prayers are said.
- Be aware that there are different interpretations of the story; some regard it as fact, others regard it as vision.

Materials
- (*not all are necessary*) OHP or flip-chart on which to write key words; a prayer mat; a picture of the Dome of the Rock in Jerusalem; some music to help children to be thoughtful or to pray; a candle.

Assembly

1. Ask the children to think about why people pray. Ask for volunteers to share their ideas. Some suggestions might be: to talk to God; to listen to God; to ask for help; to say sorry; to thank God. Write the key words on the flip-chart or OHP.

2. Explain that for Muslims, prayer is very important: five times a day they stop what they are doing and pray to God. They pray at the beginning of the day, in the middle of the day, in the late afternoon, in the evening and last thing at night. These five daily prayers are known as Salat. Before prayer, Muslims wash carefully as a way of being ready to pray and to show respect to God. Each time they pray, wherever they are in the world, they face towards Makkah, one of the most special and holiest places for Muslims.

   You could show the children the prayer mat at this point and explain that it is placed on the ground so that the top end points towards Makkah.

3. Tell the story of why prayer is so important. Muslims believe that God sent many messengers, or prophets, to earth to tell people about God and how he wanted them to live. The last messenger was the Prophet Muhammad. He was the most important messenger, and because of this Muslims give him great honour. They say a blessing after his name: 'peace be upon him'. It was the Prophet who told them of God's command to pray five times a day. At this time of year Muslims think about the story of where that command came from. It's the story of the Prophet's Night Journey and Ascension.

A long time ago, nearly 1,400 years, the Prophet Muhammad was living in Makkah, which is in the country we now call Saudi Arabia. It was a difficult and sad time for him. People would not listen to what he said about God; they were angry with him and hostile towards him. But one night, something wonderful happened. The Prophet was woken by an angel, who took him on an amazing journey. It seemed that he travelled on a mysterious animal rather like a horse with wings. When the journey was finished, the Prophet had arrived in Jerusalem. Muslims call this journey 'al-Isra', the night journey. It is why Jerusalem is a very special place for Muslims.

This wasn't the end of the journey, because then the angel took the Prophet from Jerusalem on a journey to heaven. This part of the journey is called 'al-Mi'raj', the ascension. On this second part of the journey the Prophet passed through seven heavens, where he met other prophets. Finally he met with God. It was a wonderful meeting that seemed to happen in an instant. Now the Prophet knew that God would help and guide him in the difficult time ahead. Then God commanded him to tell people about the importance of prayer. It was a way in which they could communicate with God, and they should pray to God five times a day.

The Prophet returned home, having learned many things, feeling hopeful and more able to deal with the hostility he met from those who were against him.

4. Explain that Jerusalem is a holy city for two other religions. Ask if anyone knows what which they are – Judaism and Christianity.

Add that the place in Jerusalem from which the Prophet began the second part of the journey, to heaven, can still be seen today. It is called the Dome of the Rock.

Focus on the themes

Ask the children to think again about prayer. What did God tell the Prophet that prayer was? Ask the children to think about the different ways in which people can show that they are praying. For example, hands together, eyes closed, kneeling, lighting a candle, hands raised in the air. When Muslims perform Salat (the five daily prayers), they use different positions, like standing, bowing, kneeling, or kneeling with their head touching the ground. These are different ways of showing how they feel about God and these help them to concentrate and be ready to communicate with God.

Time for reflection

Explain that there's a time now when children might like to pray or to think about what they have heard. Perhaps they would like to pray about the things that they need help with today, or to say thank you for a good thing that has happened. Perhaps they might like to use this time to think about something that is important to them.

Try to create an appropriate atmosphere for reflection by lighting a candle and playing some quiet music. Explain what you are going to do beforehand. Invite the children to change their position if it would help them. They might like to think of the positions mentioned above in which people express their feelings about God. Explain that it might help them to concentrate if they close their eyes gently.

Allow for a time of quiet and stillness. You could use the words of a prayer or poem that is well known to the children. Indicate beforehand how this time of reflection will end, either by fading the music, saying 'Amen', or using some other form of closing words. You might like to ask the children to leave in their class groups in silence with the music still gently playing, so that they can retain a sense of peacefulness.

RAMADAN

Muslim festival

Suitable for KS2

 Themes

To understand that Ramadan is a special time for Muslims; to think about what is important in life.

 Preparation and materials

Background
- Ramadan is the fourth of the 'five pillars' of Islam, the five requirements of being a Muslim. They are called 'pillars' because like pillars they support the Muslim way of life. Ramadan is marked by a fast, which lasts for the ninth month of the lunar year. It marks the time when Muslims believe their holy book, the Qur'an, was revealed to them by the Prophet Muhammad.

Materials
- A bowl of dates and a glass of milk; an empty bowl and glass. Display a collection of books or posters on Islam from your local RE Resource Centre (details of your local RE Centre can be found on the RE Directory website: www.theredirectory. org.uk).

 Assembly

1. Ask everyone to think about a month which is important for them, e.g. the month in which their birthday falls, a month in which they go on holiday, a month when spring flowers appear, the month of a religious festival. Go on to explain that there is a special month for Muslims. During this month they get up very early, before the sun rises, and eat a large

breakfast. They do not eat or drink again until the sun has set and it is dark. It's a long time to go without food or drink, from before dawn until sunset. Think about what it would be like – or what it is like for local Muslims, perhaps at your school. This time is known as Ramadan, and going without food or drink is known as fasting.

2. Explain the reasons why Muslims fast during Ramadan. By going without food and drink they remember that there are more important things in life than the needs of their bodies. Being faithful to God, or Allah as they call him, and obeying God's words are the most important things in life, so during the month of Ramadan Muslims spend more time reading from the holy book, the Qur'an, and speaking to God in prayer.

   Think about what is important in your life. Is food and drink the most important thing to you? Are the things you possess, like your toys or your clothes, the most important things to you?

3. When the sun goes down it's time to eat and drink again. Very often Muslims will break the fast by eating a few dates and drinking milk or water before they have a large family meal together.

   It's not easy to fast, so young children, elderly people, pregnant women and people who are sick don't have to, until they are older or are feeling stronger. Everyone else tries to make the effort.

   Going without food or drink during the daylight hours is also important in other ways. It's a hard thing to do and so it helps Muslims to be able to cope with the times in their lives when hard or difficult things happen.

   Feeling hungry and thirsty also helps them to understand what it is like for people in the world who do not have enough to eat or drink all the time, and so they set aside money to give to the poor. The amount they set aside equals the cost of a meal for each person in the family. So if there are five people in the family, they will give away the cost of a meal for five people. What amount might you give away in your family?

4. How might Muslims feel at Ramadan? Perhaps you could ask Muslim children to describe what it's like to keep the fast of Ramadan.

One of the things that makes fasting easier is that it's a time when Muslims feel closer to one another because they know that Muslims all over the world are going through the same experiences.

At the end of the month they have a party to celebrate. It's called the Festival of Breaking the Fast (Eid-ul-Fitr) and it's a time of great happiness and thanksgiving to God.

 Time for reflection

Take time now to think or to pray about what you've heard. You could use these words as a focus for the reflection.

Muslims at this time of year think about what is important to them. Think about what is worthwhile in your life. What gives your life meaning, what is important to you?

As Muslims think about people who do not have enough food to eat or drink, we pray for those people around the world who are hungry and thirsty all the time, because there is not enough food for them to eat, or clean water to drink.

Encourage children to say their own quiet prayers of thanks for having enough food to eat and safe, clean water to drink.

ROSH HASHANA

Jewish new year festival: September/October

Suitable for Whole School

 Aim

To explore the roots and meaning of the festival and the themes of Jewish new year. To think about new beginnings, and the effects our actions have on others.

 Preparation and materials

Background
- The festival of Rosh Hashana celebrates the beginning of the Jewish new year. It has three themes, which are woven together: celebrating the creation of the world and God as creator of the world; reflecting on behaviour, for which people will be judged by God; the relationship of God with the Jewish people.

Materials
- Bowls, some containing apple chunks and others containing honey. Some volunteers to distribute the apples and honey during or after the assembly.
- A Rosh Hashana greetings card (available from large newsagents).
- If possible, contact your nearest RE centre and see if you can borrow a *shofar* (an instrument, usually a ram's horn), which is blown at religious services during Rosh Hashana.
- A children's Bible.

 Assembly

1. Introduce the idea of new beginnings. What new things have happened so far this term? e.g. a move into a new classroom,

the arrival of new children and teachers, a new place to hang coats and bags, a new place to sit, making a new friend, learning something new.

2. Explain that for Jewish people, Rosh Hashana is the beginning of a new year. It's a time to celebrate and to think about important things. Often they wear new clothes, or their best clothes. They send cards to one another. They eat special food, for example apples dipped in honey, because they hope the new year will be filled with good and sweet things.

   You could pass the bowls around at this point, or if this threatens to be too disruptive then dip a piece of apple in the honey and eat it, and explain that there will be bowls of apple and honey to taste on the way out of the assembly.

3. During the religious services of Rosh Hashana the story is told of the birth of Isaac, and the obedience of his father Abraham, who prepares to follow God's instructions and sacrifice his son (Genesis 21—22). The latter part of this story is difficult for a short whole-school assembly and needs some background explanation. It is suggested that the first part of the story in Genesis 21 is told, using a children's Bible. This is the story of Abraham and Sarah longing for a child, God's promise to give Abraham a son and make Abraham father of a great nation, finishing with the birth of Isaac and the joy of Sarah and Abraham.

   Explain that for Sarah and Abraham, the birth of Isaac was a wonderful new beginning. It was the beginning of a new life. Explain also that even though they had waited so long and had almost given up expecting a baby, God kept his promise and Isaac was born.

   Go on to explain that at Rosh Hashana Jews celebrate the belief that God is faithful and cares for them.

4. Rosh Hashana is also a time when Jews think about the effect that their actions have on others. Use this as a way in for children to think about the effect their behaviour has on others. Think of examples together. Perhaps some are good at making people laugh. Perhaps some are friendly, helping to make someone who is lonely feel better. Perhaps some find it easy to say, or do, unkind things, and that makes people sad.

   Explain that at Rosh Hashana Jews think about their actions in the same way, and they think about how God sees

what they do. They believe that God wants them to do good
things. This is the time when they can say sorry, to God and
to others, and try and put right the things that they have done
wrong. Go on to suggest that children might like to use time
today to put right something they know they have done
wrong.

Time for reflection

At Rosh Hashana, Psalm 27 is said. Below is an adaptation of the
first verse of this psalm. You might like to read it and ask the
children to think about the words during a moment of quiet.

> God is like a light in the darkness and he saves me.
> So I need not be afraid.
> God is like a safe place.
> So I need not be afraid.

Or you could invite children to think about the following words,
or make their own prayer.

> I have been hurt by unkind words.
> I have been hurt when someone was unkind to me.
> But, I have hurt others with unkind words and I have been
> unkind to others.
> At the beginning of this new term
> may we choose to say good things and do kind things for each
> other.

Song

'Shalom, Shalom' (*Come and Praise*, 2)

SUKKOT

Jewish festival of shelters: September/October

Suitable for Whole School

Aim

To learn about the festival, focusing on two of the festival's themes: (1) remembering (the time when the Jews lived in temporary shelters in the desert after their escape from slavery in Egypt), and (2) giving thanks to God for the harvest. To build a *sukkah* (a temporary shelter).

Preparation and materials

Background

- *Sukkot* is plural for the Hebrew word *sukkah*, which has a number of meanings, including 'shelter' or 'hut'. During the festival, Jewish families and groups build sukkot (temporary shelters) outside. They often eat meals together in the sukkah, entertain friends and even sleep inside them. During Sukkot the shelters can be seen against the outside walls of houses, schools or synagogues, on the balconies of flats, or against garden sheds or climbing frames. The ceilings are decorated with branches and leaves, but with gaps to see the sky. Inside, the walls are decorated with flowers and fruit hanging from the ceiling. The sukkah is a reminder of the temporary existence of the Israelites (the ancient Jews), escaping from slavery thousands of years ago. It is a reminder of the hardship of their life in the desert and their dependence on God.
- This assembly involves a simple telling of the story of the festival. It can include the building of a sukkah, as a class or school activity, in order to illustrate the story.

Materials

- If you build a *sukkah* outside you can use playground equipment as the basic structure. Use material, sheets of paper or cardboard to fill in three sides, with one side open for the entrance. Hang paper or real flowers, fruit and vegetables from the ceiling. Make sure you can see the sky through the ceiling. Ideally it should be big enough to put a couple of chairs and a table inside. Alternatively you can make a structure in the corner of the classroom or hall.

- A children's Bible.
- *Harvest*: Sukkot is also a special time when Jews remember that everything comes from God. As a way of remembering this they say prayers of thanks to God and wave four plants in all directions: a citrus fruit or branch, palm leaves, myrtle, and willow. These plants represent the harvest. Children could do some research in advance and draw pictures of them.

Assembly

1. Ask if any of the children have ever slept outside. Perhaps they've been on an organized camp with other children, or on a camping holiday with their families. Ask them to think of single words that describe the feeling of sleeping 'outside', e.g. cold, scary, lonely, exciting.

2. Using a children's Bible tell the story of the Exodus from the point where the Israelites have escaped from slavery in Egypt and begin their journey through the desert to their new homeland (Exodus 15.22—17.16). Include the story of how God provides their food (manna) and water. You will need to remind them that Moses was their leader.

3. Follow up the issues raised in the story. What must it have been like to journey through the desert? Explain that the desert can be very hot during the day, but very cold at night. There are often wild animals living there. Is it easy to understand why the people grumbled at first? Talk about how God provided food and water for them – how might they have felt when they saw how God was taking care of them?

4. Explain how every year Jews build temporary shelters outside, called *sukkahs*, to celebrate the way in which God looked after their ancestors all those years ago. They call the festival Sukkot, the name for lots of sukkahs. Refer to the one you have built together. Adapt the background information.

In the sukkahs the Jews eat meals together. Sometimes they sleep in them. It is a time to be happy.

 Time for reflection

> Dear God,
> Thank you for the food we have to eat and the fresh, clean water we have to drink.
> Thank you for our homes where we can shelter from the rain and the cold.
> We pray for all those people who will not have enough food to eat today,
> or homes to live in.
> **Amen.**

If you have built a sukkah, small groups could visit it at different times during the day and have something to eat inside. Or you could leave the sukkah in place for a while as a quiet space for children to think and pray.

HANUKAH

Jewish festival of light: November/December

Suitable for Whole School or Class Assembly

 Themes

Standing up for what is important; overcoming difficulty; light.

 Preparation and materials

- If possible borrow a Hanukah lamp (*hanukiyah*) or find a picture of one. Your local RE Resource Centre may be able to help (details of your local RE Centre can be found on the RE Directory website: www.theredirectory.org.uk).
- Display a plate of doughnuts or traditional Jewish potato pancakes cooked in oil (*latkes*).

 Assembly

1. Ask the children to imagine that something very special to them is deliberately broken or spoilt by someone. How would they feel?

   Explain that at this time of year Jews all over the world celebrate a festival called Hanukah. During the festival they remember a story from long ago in which something very special to the Jews was taken from them and spoilt, and how God helped them. Tell the following story.

2. The story happened a long time ago, over 2,000 years. For the Jews their most special place was the temple in Jerusalem. It was special because it was holy – they believed that they could meet with God there. But the temple was captured by the King of Syria, Antiochus Epiphanes. He didn't want the Jews to follow their own beliefs or to worship God in the way they wanted to. Instead, King Antiochus wanted the Jews to obey him and to worship the Greek gods that he

worshipped. He captured the temple, destroyed everything inside it and put up statues of Greek gods. Imagine how it must have felt for the Jews to see their most special place spoilt and in ruins.

Then a group of men decided that they would stand up against the King and defend what was important to them. They lived in caves in the hills near Jerusalem and from there they launched attacks on the armies of King Antiochus. Their leader was called Judas Maccabeus. People said he was brave, a clear thinker and someone who would not give up. This band of men (which also included Judas's brothers) had a name: the Maccabees (or 'hammers').

Eventually the Maccabees managed to clear the temple in Jerusalem of their enemies, but they were left with the sad sight of the destruction that had been caused. The gates had been burned, bushes had started to grow inside, and animals wandered through the ruins. So the Maccabees rebuilt the temple and they announced a day when the temple would be open again and they could pray to God.

It was a great day of singing and music and thanksgiving to God. One of the most important parts of the celebrations that day was to re-light a huge candlestick with eight branches, called a menora, which was kept burning in the temple as a sign of God's everlasting presence. The menora was fuelled with special oil, but when the people searched for the oil all they could find was one small jar, with only enough oil for a single night.

They lit the menora, expecting the light to go out when the oil burned down, but instead when they returned the next day there was still some oil left over and the light continued to burn. For eight whole days the oil from the one small jar lasted, until new oil supplies arrived. The Jews knew that a great miracle had happened on the site of their temple and that God had helped them in times of great danger and difficulty.

3. From that time on the Jews have celebrated the time when their temple that had been vandalized and spoilt was rebuilt. They call the celebrations Hanukah and they last for eight days, just like the oil did. It's a festival that's full of light. Each day they light a lamp called a *hanukiyah* to remind them

of the story of the Maccabees and the miraculous supply of oil. They say special prayers and give thanks to God.

Show the children the *hanukiyah*. Explain that there are eight individual lamps or candles and a servant candle (*shamash*) with its own holder slightly apart from the eight branches. On the first evening of Hanukah the candle on the extreme right is lit using the servant candle. At the end of the evening the two candles are extinguished. On the seven nights that follow the next unlit candle along the row is lit first (using the servant candle) and then the candles from the previous nights are re-lit. Those who like numbers might like to calculate how many times candles are lit on the *hanukiyah* over the eight nights (answer 44, i.e. $1 + 1$, $+ 1 + 2$, $+ 1 + 3$, $+ 1 + 4$, and so on).

4. Hanukah is a time of family celebrations too. Games are played and food that is cooked in oil is eaten. (Show the children the doughnuts and *latkes*. You may like to cut them into portions and distribute them after the assembly.) It's a time of great hope. The story of the Maccabees helps Jews to face the future with courage, even when things are difficult.

Focus on the themes

Think about what is important. What would you be prepared to protect and stand up for: your family, your friends, your home, your beliefs?

Time for reflection

Encourage the children to be still and to think or pray about the things they have heard. Light some candles as a visual focus. You could use some of these phrases to help.

God of all,
Thank you that we are free to follow our own beliefs.
We think of people in the world who are not free:
people who are hated or laughed at because of what they
    believe.
Help us to be ready to understand and listen to people we meet,
even if we do not agree with them.

THE BIRTHDAY OF GURU NANAK

Sikh festival: October/November

Note: The birth date of Guru Nanak was 15 April 1469, but popular tradition encouraged celebrations later in the year.

Suitable for KS2

 ### Themes

The life of Guru Nanak; equality; leadership.

 ### Preparation and materials

Background
- Guru Nanak lived from 1469 to 1539 CE. He was the founder of the Sikh religion.

Materials
- A map of the world with India highlighted.
- A bowl of rice.

 ### Assembly

1. Ask the children to think about the word 'leader'. What leaders have they heard about? Ask for a few suggestions. Talk about why people become leaders: e.g. they are chosen by people, like a prime minister or a leader (captain) of a sports team; they use force to become leaders and keep themselves in power like a dictator; they feel inspired or called by God, like a religious leader.
2. Think about what it takes to be a good leader. What sort of person would you choose to lead you? Here are some suggestions: someone who is trustworthy; someone who is believable; someone who can make a difference and change things for the good; someone who cares for people.
3. Explain that today you are thinking about a great leader

called Guru Nanak. Guru means teacher, and people who follow Guru Nanak's teaching are called Sikhs. He was a great leader, not because he had a big army, or because he was very strong, but because he taught people about God. The things he had to say about God were so amazing that people wanted to follow him and learn more about God.

4. Tell the following story:

There are many stories told about Guru Nanak. He was born over 500 years ago in northern India. (*Point to it on the map if you have one available.*)

He lived at a time when there was much argument between people because they believed different things about God.

When Guru Nanak was a child people thought he was a dreamer and that he was only interested in writing poetry. His father gave him some money to start a business, but Guru Nanak met some people who were hungry and he used the money to buy food for them. This made his father very angry, but Guru Nanak said that it was more important to feed hungry people.

One day he went for a swim in a river. He swam under the water, but he didn't come up again. People gathered to look for him. They could see his clothes lying by the side of the river, but there was no movement in the water. Soon people began to think that he had drowned. They were sad because they remembered his kindness and his honesty.

Three days passed. People had given up hope of ever seeing Nanak again. Then suddenly Nanak appeared at his home. His family and his friends were so pleased to see him, but something about him had changed. His eyes seemed to be brighter and his face was full of happiness. Then he explained that when he was in the river he had seen a vision of God and God had told him to give people a message. The message was that God has made everything and loves everyone. God doesn't see the differences that we see between us, he sees us as equals and he wants us all to live peacefully with one another.

From that time on people started to call Nanak 'Guru', or teacher. Guru Nanak gave all that he had to the poor and he made four long journeys to tell people the message God had given him in the river. At this time of year Sikhs all over the world celebrate the birth of Guru Nanak.

5. During the festival there are often processions through the street and firework displays. In the Sikh temples, which are called *gurdwaras*, the Sikh holy book, called the Guru Granth Sahib, is read from beginning to end. In the Punjab in India, where the Sikh religion began, children are given new clothes and have the day off school to join in the celebrations. Candles are lit in the gurdwara and in homes, shops and offices.

 ## Focus on the themes

Think about the things that make us different from one another, e.g. the way we look, the clothes we wear, how much money we have, the food we eat, the hobbies we have, the football teams we support, the things we believe. How do we react when we meet someone who is different? What did Guru Nanak teach about the differences between us? He taught that God is not interested in the differences between us, whether we're big or small, strong or weak, and that everyone is equal.

 ## Time for reflection

Take time now to think or to pray about some of the things you have heard today. You could use these words to help you.

Some of us are big, some are small.
Some are strong, some are weak.
Some are old and some are young.
Some are rich and some are poor.

It's easy to ignore people when they seem different from us. It's easy to laugh at people who seem different from us. It's easy to fight with people who seem different from us.

Guru Nanak said that we are equal because we are created and loved by God. Help us to treat each other as equals.

VAISAKHI (or BAISAKHI)

Sikh new year festival: April

Suitable for a Whole School or Class Assembly

 Themes

Loyalty, self-sacrifice, devotion, bravery.

 Preparation and materials

Background
- Vaisakhi is a new year festival in the Sikh calendar and recalls the institution of the 'Khalsa'. The story originates in 1699, after a long period of Sikh persecution. Guru Gobind Singh, the tenth and last human Guru (the Sikh holy book, the 'Guru Granth Sahib', is considered to be the last Guru), called together all the Sikhs and, as the story shows, instituted a group of five men known as the Khalsa who would be willing to dedicate themselves to God, to defend their faith and to care for the poor and the helpless.
- From this time onwards men and women from as young as 16 or 18 have been initiated into the Khalsa as a sign of their commitment to follow the Sikh way of life.
- On Vaisakhi people gather in *gurdwaras* (temples) and there is a continuous reading of the Guru Granth Sahib. A new Sikh flag is put in place and the flag pole washed. There are shared meals and celebrations. Very often people are initiated into the Khalsa on this day.

Materials
- If possible, find pictures of some of the five 'K's – the five symbols of those who have dedicated themselves to the Sikh way of life. These are: uncut hair (*kesh*); the hair comb used to keep the hair clean and neat (*kanga*); a steel wrist-band which, through its unbroken circle, reminds Sikhs that God is one (*kara*); the sword, which symbolizes the willingness to defend

the faith and the poor and helpless (*kirpan*); and short trousers (*kacha*). You might also like to mention the Sikh turban, which is not one of the five Ks but is used to keep the uncut hair (*kesh*) tidy. This is a good opportunity to invite a Sikh parent or a representative from the Sikh community along to show the five Ks and to talk about the festival.

- On a board you could put some of the key words from the assembly, such as devotion, Guru, Sikh, etc.
- A picture of the Sikh flag.

Assembly

1. Introduce the theme of devotion. What are children devoted to? Football teams? Pop bands? How do we show our devotion to things? Wearing football scarves, buying the CDs of the bands we like; going to church or to the temple. Explain that today's assembly is about a group of people who showed their devotion to God in an amazing way. Explain that the story is important for Sikhs who celebrate a festival known as Vaisakhi at this time.

2. The story comes from India. It happened a long time ago, over 300 years. For the Sikhs life was difficult. They had been under attack for many years. There were lots of poor people without anyone to help them.

    The Sikh leader was called Guru Gobind Singh. Guru means teacher, and he taught people about God. Guru Gobind Singh decided things had to change, and so, on the spring festival of Vaisakhi, he called the Sikhs to join him. There was a huge crowd, over 20,000 people. Guru Gobind Singh stood outside his tent and called out: 'I need a Sikh who is willing to die for God and for the Guru.'

    His words were passed through the crowd. Everyone was amazed. Who was devoted enough to give up their life? Twice more the Guru called out to the crowd and asked the question. Then one man came forward. Guru Gobind Singh took him into his tent. After a while the Guru came out by himself. But in his hand was a sword covered in blood! The crowd gasped. Then the Guru asked again. 'Who is willing to die for God and the Guru?' Surely no one else would come forward.

    What about that sword with blood on the blade? But then

another man stepped forward and went into the tent with the Guru. Once again the Guru came out of the tent alone, with blood on his sword. Then amazingly, another man stepped forward and went into the tent, and then another. Four brave and devoted men – and each time the Guru stepped out of the tent alone, with his sword in his hand.

Then a fifth man stepped forward and went into the tent with the Guru. How many men must die, the crowd wondered. But this time the Guru came out of the tent, with his sword, and behind him were the five men. They were still alive!

'This was a test,' the Guru explained, 'to see who was brave enough and willing to give up everything to show how much they were devoted to God.' The Guru called the five men the 'Panje Pyare', the beloved ones. They were to become the first members of a group called the Khalsa, which would defend the Sikh faith and care for the poor and helpless, whoever they were and whatever they believed.

Then the Guru made a mixture of sugar and water called 'amrit'. He asked the beloved ones to give him some of the amrit, to show that although he was the Guru, all people were equal in God's eyes. That day amrit was given to people in the crowd who said that they believed in one God, and that all people were equal. They were given new last names too, to show that they now belonged to one big family – women were given the name Kaur, which means princess, and men were given the name Singh, which means lion.

3. From that time onwards any man or woman, or boy or girl, who shows that they want to follow the Sikh way of life, takes part in a special ceremony which is often celebrated at this time. They, too, join the Khalsa and they make five important promises:

1 To wear five signs or symbols of the faith (see the five K's above).
2 To follow the teachings of the Sikh Gurus and the holy book called the Guru Granth Sahib.
3 To help people in need.
4 To give up alcohol and tobacco and to be faithful to their husbands or wives.
5 To work hard and to give to charity.

Stress that the point of the festival is not that the five wanted to die for their beliefs, but that Sikhs wish to serve God and people in a peaceful and helpful way.

Focus on the themes

Think again about what you are devoted to. Is it so important to you that you would give up everything for it? Is it worth being devoted to – will it bring happiness, will it last, will it help people?

Time for reflection

Invite the children to take part in a time of quiet and to think about what they have heard. Use music to help the reflection. You could go on to say the following words which are adapted from those said by the fifth Guru, Guru Arjan:

> 'Not even the scorching wind touches him who takes refuge in the Lord.
> He throws his protective ring around us so that no suffering can overpower us.
> How fortunate we are that God is our support.'

BODHI DAY

Buddhist festival: December

Suitable for KS2

 Themes

To learn about how the Buddha gained enlightenment. To understand how learning something new can change the way we think about things. The place of suffering in learning and growth.

 Preparation and materials

Background
- The dates and celebration of Buddhist festivals vary greatly. Not all Buddhists will celebrate the same festival. Bodhi day is celebrated by Pure Land Buddhists, who are mainly found in Japan and the United States. Buddhism is practised all around the world but is particularly found in Sri Lanka, Burma, Thailand, Tibet, China and South Korea. Similar festivals celebrating the birth, enlightenment and death of the Buddha fall for the majority of the world's Buddhists in May.

Materials
- A picture of a Bodhi tree (see the website www.buddhanet.net) or a large drawing of a fig leaf; a picture of the Buddha sitting cross-legged; a candle or some object that could be a focus for the reflection, e.g. a flower.

 Assembly

1. Explain that today is an important day for many Buddhists – people who follow the teachings of a man who became known as the Buddha. Buddha means 'enlightened one', or the one who has a special understanding of things, someone who knows what is important.

2. Talk in general about 'knowing'. Explain that all of us know lots of things. We know how to play games, we know how to put on our coats, we know that running into the road is dangerous. Talk about some of the other things we know, perhaps relating this to recent school topics. Go on to say that we know many things, but of course there are many things that we don't know too.

   But the Buddha came to know something very different from all the things mentioned above. He recognized that in life things do not always go the way we want them to. However much we know, things still go wrong. People get ill, people are hungry, there are wars, people steal from one another or are unhappy and everything in life comes to an end.

   Buddhists believe that the Buddha came to know about what causes suffering and unhappiness and what can be done about it. This was the special understanding or 'enlightenment' that the Buddha received. Go on to tell the story of how the Buddha reached enlightenment.

3. The Buddha was born a long time ago – about 2,500 years ago. The Buddha was not the name he was given at birth. His birth name was Siddhartha Gautama and he was a prince. He was born in a part of the world that we now call Nepal (the country that has the highest mountains in the world). Siddhartha's father wanted to protect his son and so Siddhartha grew up in the palace grounds. He never went outside the grounds, and had no idea what life was really like for most people. He had a rich and happy life, with everything he could possibly want: food to eat, clothes to wear, and when he was old enough he married a beautiful girl and they had a son. But still Siddhartha had not seen anything of life outside the palace grounds.

   Soon he began to grow bored with his sheltered life and one day he left the palace. Now he began to see the world as it really was. As he rode around he saw suffering everywhere. He saw an old man who was weak and nearly at the end of his life. He saw a man who was sick and in great pain, and he saw a funeral with the family of the dead man crying around his body.

   Then Siddhartha came across a holy man, a man who had devoted his life to following God. This man seemed to be happy and peaceful.

These things made Siddhartha think. He went back to the palace, but he couldn't forget what he had seen. He decided he had to go in search of the answer to why there was suffering in the world. On the night before his 29th birthday he left his palace with its riches, beauty and safety. He left behind his beautiful robes and put on the simple clothes worn by holy men and shaved off all his hair just like the holy man he had seen.

For the next six years he travelled around the country in search of the answer to the question of why there is suffering in the world, but he could not find the answer. He travelled on until he came to a great tree. Today we call this tree a Bodhi tree. It's like a fig tree. He sat under this great big tree and began to meditate, that is to think deeply. It was the night of a full moon. After a long time, the truth came to him, and discovering the truth gave Siddhartha a feeling of great peacefulness. It was a feeling of release from all the things that had been troubling him. Suddenly he was able to stop thinking about himself and his worries. Siddhartha had become enlightened – he had found truth and so he became known as the Buddha – the enlightened one.

The Buddha learned many things while meditating under the Bodhi tree and he spent the rest of his life teaching people about what he had learned so that they might find peace in their own lives. One of the things he discovered is that very often people make themselves and others unhappy because they are always wanting and needing things. They are tied to the things they need and want, like a dog tied to a tree. The more they want the more they get tied up in knots, like the dog getting tangled in the rope that attaches it to the tree. The Buddha taught his followers about how they could be free of the things that tie them down and how this would give them peace and happiness. He taught them that they could become enlightened too by following his teachings.

 ### Focus on the themes

Explain that this story explains why today many Buddhists celebrate Bodhi day, the day that the Buddha achieved enlightenment under the Bodhi tree.

Think about the dog tied to the tree. Ask the children to think of themselves as the dog. What are the things or behaviour or desires that spoil someone's life and keep them tied up like the dog? e.g. always wanting what others have, being unkind to others, trying to be better than others. The children might like to draw this as a picture after the assembly with the dog tied to a tree in the middle of a page and all the things that tie them down around the outside. You could do this as a full assembly activity with the dog and tree represented on an OHP surrounded by suggestions from children about the things that tie them down and make them unhappy.

 ## Time for reflection

Ask the children to sit quietly. Explain that the Buddha is often seen sitting quietly, cross-legged, meditating. By sitting quietly and breathing deeply he was able to clear his mind of all the things that worried him and focus on the things that were important. Explain that this is what Buddhists do today. Very often they focus on a particular object in front of them, usually something beautiful like a flower. Invite the children to do the same. Ask them to sit as quietly as possible. Give them time to find a comfortable position. Suggest that if they would like to they can close their eyes, or they can look at the focus object you have put out for them. Explain that there will be a time of complete quiet in which no words will be said. Invite them to try to clear their minds of all the things that they're thinking about or worried about, and to focus instead on the object in front of them. If they find this difficult, suggest that they just keep as still as possible and enjoy the quiet all around them. Indicate how they will know that the time of silence has come to an end, e.g. by blowing out the candle, or covering the focus object.

Keep silence for as long as is comfortable. At the end you could suggest that the children talk to their friends and teachers after the assembly about the experience of trying to meditate. What was it like, how did they feel, was it a difficult thing to do, was it helpful to be still and silent? Explain that it does take a lot of practice. They could discuss how noisy our world is and think about why many people believe that being quiet and still helps them to cope with the busy, noisy world.

Note: A useful resource on using silence to develop children's spiritual awareness is *Don't Just Do Something, Sit There* by Mary K. Stone (RMEP, ISBN 1085175-105-X).

CHINESE NEW YEAR, OR YUAN TAN

Chinese spring festival: January/February

Suitable for a KS2 or Class Assembly

 Themes

Chinese New Year; new beginnings; looking forward to the future.

 Preparation and materials

Background

- Chinese New Year is a spring festival and has been celebrated for over 3,000 years. Originally it was a festival in which farmers hoped for a good harvest in the year to come. It is linked to the lunar calendar and the first day of the New Year always has a new moon.
- In China, every year has the name of an animal. There are 12 important animals, so each one has its turn once every 12 years. The animals are: rat, ox, tiger, rabbit, dragon, snake, horse, ram, monkey, rooster, dog, pig.
- Before the festival there is a period of preparation when houses are cleaned, lucky red decorations are hung over doors and around rooms, and new clothes are bought. Debts and business accounts are settled before New Year's Day. Ancestor worship is very important in Chinese culture and the period before New Year is especially a time to remember ancestors.
- The festival can last up to 15 days, but is usually celebrated over three days. Shops and businesses are usually shut and people gather in family groups and visit friends. It's a time of religious reflection and great fun with the giving of gifts, flowers, sweets and lucky money, as well as feasting, dragon dances and fireworks.

Materials

- A picture of the animal of the New Year; a traditional Chinese red envelope for lucky money; a picture of a dragon dance or a dragon mask. Show these at appropriate times in the assembly.

Assembly

1. Remind the children of the new year celebrations they may have had this year. What did they do? Using the background material, explain that for many Chinese people today is the first day of their new year. They've been looking forward to it over the last few weeks and getting their houses ready for the celebrations. These preparations include putting up big red decorations (red is thought to be a lucky colour), hanging two-line messages with new year good wishes around the doors, cleaning the house and buying new clothes. It's also a time when Chinese people visit their temples and they especially remember their ancestors, people who were part of the family but who have now died. Explain that for many Chinese people respect for parents and for elderly people is very important.

2. Explain that today, the first day of the new year, everyone wishes everyone else 'Happy New Year' – much as we do on 1 January. It's a time to be thankful for the last year, to look forward to what may happen this year and to hope that it will be a good one. Children are given special little red envelopes (remember that red is a lucky colour) with 'lucky money' inside. Families will meet together to eat special food and wear new clothes. In some places dumplings are a favourite new year food and they have different fillings, each of which have a different meaning: for example, dumplings filled with sugar will bring a sweet life. Sometimes there's money inside the dumplings.

3. Explain that there are also things that you can't do on Chinese New Year's Day. Knives and scissors are not used because they are thought to be unlucky. So if you need a hair-cut, you must have it done before the New Year festival! During this time everyone tries to be kind and friendly to everyone else.

4. Point out that animals are very important too. Every year has the name of an animal. There are 12 important animals, so each animal has its turn once every 12 years. Many people

think that the sort of person you are – your personality – depends on the year you were born. For instance, rams (2003) are thought to be kind and to take care of their families, but sometimes they can't make up their minds.

5. Explain that the celebrations will go on after today. Chinese New Year can be a noisy time too, because people light firecrackers. A long time ago this was thought to chase away ghosts and monsters.

There's lots of dancing too. People get together in teams for these dances. One of the most well-known is the dragon dance, where one person wears a dragon mask, and the people following on behind, under a long piece of cloth, are the dragon's tail. There can be twenty or thirty people inside the tail. Dragons were thought to be friendly and helpful and that's why people dress up as dragons today.

Focus on the themes

Recap on the things that are important in Chinese New Year: spending time with family and friends, being kind to one another, hoping for enough food to eat and enough money to live on, remembering people who have died. Ask the children what they think might make a good new year.

Time for reflection

Prepare the children for a time of quiet. Invite them to sit comfortably and to close their eyes if it helps them to concentrate. Play music or light a candle to signify that this is a special time.

You could read out the following Chinese wish of hope for the future: 'May your happiness be as wide as the East Sea.'

Go on to invite the children to think about two things that they hope for for their friends and family this year and two good things that they hope for for the world this year.

RIDVAN

Baha'i festival: 21 April–2 May

Suitable for a Whole School or Class Assembly

 Themes

Oneness of mankind, unity, the global family, belonging.

 Preparation and materials

Background

- The Baha'i faith is the youngest of the world's religions. It was founded by Bahá'u'lláh (1817–1892), and his followers regarded him as the most recent of God's messengers, including Abraham, Moses, Buddha, Zoroaster, Christ and Muhammad. The Baha'i faith is centred on the idea that all people belong to one human family and that the time has come to recognize this and to work for the unity of all people. The faith grew out of the Shi'ite branch of Islam in Iran. The coming of Bahá'u'lláh was announced by a young Iranian called 'The Bab'.
- The festival of Ridvan (pronounced Rizwan) is significant because it celebrates the time when Bahá'u'lláh officially announced that he was the prophet proclaimed by the Bab. The festival takes its name from the garden on the outskirts of Baghdad in which this happened. It became known as the Garden of Ridvan (paradise).

Materials

- A globe.
- A picture of a middle-eastern garden.
- A board on which to write key words like Bahia, Bahá'u'lláh, etc.

Assembly

1. Introduce the idea of belonging. What do children feel they belong to? Give examples such as school, Brownies, Cubs, a family, a class.

   What does it mean to belong? Share some ideas together, such as: to do the same things together; to have the same purpose; to care for the people to whom we feel we belong; to feel welcomed by others. How do you feel if you don't belong?

2. Explain that today's assembly is about a man who came to tell people that they belonged to one another, that they were part of one big family – the human family. His name was Bahá'u'lláh. Refer to the globe and introduce the idea that Bahá'u'lláh said this human family lives in different places, wears different clothes and eats different food, but that it belongs together because it lives in the same world.

   Explore what it means to belong to the human family. What do we have in common with one another?

3. Invite six children up to the front. Ask them to stand in a circle and hold hands. Now invite another child up to the front. Tell the one child (without anyone else hearing) that when you say 'Go', he or she must try and get into the circle of six children. Now tell the six children (without letting anyone else hear) that when you say 'Go', they must try and prevent the one child from getting into their circle, but they must not let go of each other's hands.

   Say the word 'Go'. You don't need to let what happens go on for too long, but the point is to establish what it is like when someone is prevented from 'belonging'.

4. Invite children to comment on what happened and to think about what it must have felt like for the one child to be prevented from belonging. Ask the child to describe how they felt.

   Go on to explain that Bahá'u'lláh said the time had come for people to stop fighting and disagreeing and to recognize that they were one big family, created and loved by one God.

   The followers of Bahá'u'lláh are known as Baha'is. At this time they celebrate the day on which Bahá'u'lláh began to tell people that he had been chosen by God to give this important message. The celebration is known as Ridvan, named after the garden outside Baghdad in Iraq where this happened. Ridvan means paradise. The Baha'is, the followers of Bahá'u'lláh, have often been criticized and have suffered because of their beliefs.

 ## Focus on the themes

Invite the children to think about the idea of us belonging together because we are all human and live in one world. If this is so, how does it mean we should treat one another?

 ## Time for reflection

Invite the children to keep a time of quiet. You could use these words as a prayer.

God of all,
Thank you for the world you have made.
Thank you for all the different people who live in it.
We are sorry for the times we forget that we belong to one
    human family.
Help us to care for one another.
Amen.

Other Themes

THE GOOSE WITH THE GOLDEN EGGS

By Jude Scrutton

Suitable for Whole School

 Aim

To think about the fable and its message of the power of greed.

 Preparation and materials

- You will need: an assortment of large egg shapes, painted gold; a basket for the eggs; a big plastic knife.
- Prepare children to take part in reading the script: Countryman, Goose, Narrator. They will need some time to practise the script.

 Assembly

1. Welcome the children, and explain that they will be seeing a short play based on a fable written a long time ago by someone called Aesop. Aesop was born as a slave in ancient Greece, and became a philosopher who taught people by telling them fables – stories that give you something to think about.

   Ask the children if they know any of Aesop's fables. Ask them to think, while the story is being performed, about what Aesop was trying to teach people in this story.
2. Perform the play.

   The Goose with the Golden Eggs

Narrator	One day there was a Countryman who owned a Goose. Every day the man would walk to his farm to collect the eggs that his Goose had laid.
Countryman	I wonder how many she's laid today.
Narrator	The Countryman had many bills to pay and four mouths to feed in his family. He was very

	poor but he had always been able to sell enough eggs to keep his family happy. But he wished for more.
Countryman	I want to be rich. I want to be able to afford lots of lovely things.
Narrator	That day he couldn't find any eggs at all. He looked at the Goose crossly.
Countryman	You lazy Goose! Where are my eggs? If you don't lay me any eggs I don't know what I should do!
Narrator	Just then, a glint caught his eye. Underneath the Goose he could see something shiny. He moved the Goose out of the way and there he found an egg, golden and glittering. He picked it up and was shocked to find it was heavy as lead. He shouted at the Goose, for he thought he had been tricked.
Countryman	This is no good! What have you laid for me?
Narrator	He was about to throw the egg away, then decided to take it home. To his delight he found that it was an egg made out of pure gold. Every morning the same thing happened and soon he was very rich.
	However, the richer he became, the more gold he wanted. And he wanted it *now*! An idea began to form in his mind.
Countryman	How can I get all of my money, now? Hold on, I've got an idea!
Narrator	The man took the biggest knife he could find and began to walk to his farm. The Goose, on seeing the man and his knife, began to shake in fear. In one swift move the man cut the Goose in half. He opened it up, hoping to find lots of golden eggs inside. Did he find any? Can you guess?

3. Ask the children what the moral of the story is – greed will outdo us. Direct them towards the idea that the Countryman got so greedy that he killed his source of income.
4. Ask them to think about times when they have been greedy

(eaten too much, or complained about not getting enough presents, or not being allowed the latest PlayStation game, etc.). Then ask them to think about children who are not as fortunate as themselves, children who do not have enough to eat, for example.

 Time for reflection

Lord, help us to be thankful for the things we have.
Help us to enjoy life as it is,
not wanting more and more like the Countryman in the story.
Please help us not to be greedy.
Amen.

 Song

'He made me' (*Come and Praise*, 18)

THE SUN AND THE WIND

By Jude Scrutton

Suitable for Whole School

Aim

To think about the idea that persuasiveness can be more effective than force.

Preparation and materials

- This assembly includes a short play script that will need preparation by a group of children in advance.
- *Cast*: Narrator, North Wind, Sun, Man (or could be woman).
- *Props*: The characters could hold the following props: a large cloud made out of white card, to represent the wind (to look like it is scudding along), and a large orange sun made out of card (e.g. using yellow and orange tissue paper). A coat is needed for 'Man' to put on and zip up.
- You will also need a flip-chart or OHP for listing ideas in the final section.

Assembly

1. Welcome the children and introduce the theme for the assembly – the retelling of a fable by Aesop.

   Discuss who Aesop was. He was born as a slave, but became a philosopher who taught people by telling them fables. Ask the children if they know any of his fables – can they remember any from previous assemblies? Tell the children that today's fable is different, as the story does not use animals – the characters are the sun and the wind. Ask the children to think about the meaning of the story – what was Aesop trying to teach people?

2. Perform the play:

Narrator	One day the North Wind and the Sun got into a heated discussion.
North Wind	Don't be so silly, of course I am much stronger than you.
Sun	No, you're not. It is I who am stronger than you.
Narrator	This argument continued for some time, and still they could not reach a friendly solution!
Sun	Prove that you are stronger than me.
North Wind	Easy! You see that man over there?
Narrator	The Sun and Wind looked towards a man digging and planting seeds in his garden.
Man	It's a bit cold. I think I'll wear my coat (*he puts on a winter coat*).
Sun	I see him.
North Wind	I bet I am so strong I can force that man to take off his coat.
Sun	I bet I can too! OK, you first.
Narrator	The North Wind conjured up a forceful gust.
Man	It's getting really cold. I think I'll pull up my zip.
Narrator	The North Wind, seeing the man do up his coat, blew even harder to try to force the coat off, but the man kept his coat on.
North Wind	It's no use, it won't budge. But if I can't do it, you won't!
Sun	You just watch.
Narrator	The sun began to shine with gentle warmth that made the man take off his jacket straight away.
Man	British weather, always changing.
Narrator	The sun began to shine with all its heat until the man in the garden stripped off to just his bathing suit and went off to swim in a nearby river (*child should walk off at this point as if about to take off his/her top clothes*).

3. After the play ask the children what the meaning of the story was. Value all their ideas.

   Ask them to think about times when they have used force.

List them on the flip-chart. Ask them what might have happened if they had used 'warmth' or kindness.

Finally, ask the children to think about what they might do instead of using force in the future.

 ## Time for reflection

Lord,
Help us always to stop and think,
before we use force,
let us consider warmth.
Kind words and deeds
will help us achieve
and make a new start
where force breaks apart.
Amen.

 ## Song

'By brother sun' (*Come and Praise*, 78)
'Magic Penny' (*Let's Sing*, 2)

WATER OF LIFE

By the Revd Alan M. Barker

Suitable for Whole School

 Aim

To reflect upon the importance of water and to be aware of the needs of those without clean water supplies.

 Preparation and materials

- Some wet-weather gear (*optional*). A rainy day would also be a useful aid!
- Two bottles, one filled with clean water and the other with muddy water.
- A bucket, preferably metal.
- Children could be asked to lead the Time for reflection.

 Assembly

1. Sing the first verse of 'Thank you Lord for this fine day' (*Come and Praise*, 32). Refer to the weather. If it is fine, remind the assembly that not all days are dry. Sometimes it is 'wet and horrible', but we should be thankful for rain.

   Sing 'Thank you Lord for rainy days'. Some children could wear wet-weather clothing, and perhaps parade at the front of the assembly. Or this role could be adopted by the staff!
2. Invite the children to consider why we should say 'thank you' for rain, e.g. plants need it to grow, we need water to drink, it's fun to splash in puddles!
3. Remind the assembly how water is easily obtained and 'on tap'. Water mains and pipes bring water to our homes from reservoirs and treatment plants.

   We can also buy clean bottled water. Show the children the

prepared bottles. Who would want to drink the muddy water? No one. However, many people in the world have no choice but to drink polluted water.

4. Invite the children to imagine that they are the 12-year-old girl living in Ghana in the following story.

Napoga is 12 years old. She lives in a small village in Northern Ghana, a country in Africa. In Ghana it doesn't rain for months and months. From October to June it is the dry season.

You could pause at this point to ask if any of the children have lived in other climates.

Every morning in the dry season, Napoga is woken by the sunshine and the sound of singing birds. But until recently Napoga didn't feel like singing. She couldn't go to school because there was so much work to do. As the girl in her family it was Napoga's job to fetch the water that they needed to drink and cook with. The water was in a muddy hole about half a mile from the village.

At this point you could ask the children how much water would their own families need each day. And how much water could they carry at a time?

Napoga's family used as little water as they could, but still she had to carry 8 buckets of water a day in the hot sun all the way back from the water hole. Napoga, like many Ghanaian children, had learned to carry things, not by hand, but by balancing them carefully on her head.

Perhaps pause to demonstrate using the bucket – do any children have this skill?

Napoga grew very tired. As the dry season went on, the water in the pool dried up, and she had to patiently scoop it up a little at a time, into her bucket. Often she had to wait her turn while others collected the water they needed. It would sometimes take her 6 hours each day to fetch water. Even then, the water was dirty and sometimes made her family ill. When, at last, the rains were due, Napoga's father planted seeds to grow plants for food. But if the rains didn't last long enough the young plants died. Her family were sometimes afraid that they might not have enough to eat.

So imagine the excitement Napoga felt when she heard

that their village was to have a new well. A village meeting was held and lots of plans were made. Some time later, a Land Rover and a lorry arrived, carrying cement, tools and digging equipment. Everyone in the village worked together to dig the well. Eventually it was deep enough and it began to fill with water. The work went on until the deep hole was covered and all Napoga could see was a concrete base with a hand-pump to draw the water from far below the ground.

One of the men of the village pumped the handle, and clean water gushed out (pour some of the clean bottled water from a height into the bucket).

Napoga cheered. Her family cheered! Her friends cheered! Everyone cheered! They knew that the new supply of water would change their lives.

Can the children think how?

So now when Napoga wakes, she sings with the birds. She doesn't have to spend so much time collecting water and can play with her friends and go to the local school in the village. Her father can use some of the water to help his crops grow so that the family won't be hungry. And her mother can use clean water for cooking and Napoga and her friends won't get upset tummies any more.

5. Reflect that often we take for granted all the water we use every day. Refer the children to organizations such as Water Aid (www.wateraid.org.uk) which assist some of the world's poorest people to gain access to clean water supplies.

 Time for reflection

Creator God,
You make springs flow in the valleys and rivers run between the hills.
From the sky you send rain on the hills
and the earth is filled with your blessings.

Today we thank you for your gift of rain, that helps plants to grow,
and makes rivers flow.
We thank you for clean water,

which we can drink,
and which keeps us healthy.
Amen.

 Song

'Water of life' (*Come and Praise*, 2)

RULES FOR LIFE

By the Revd Guy Donegan-Cross

Suitable for Whole School

 Aim

To show how rules at school and in life help us to grow and flourish. To explore the idea that rules need to be kept, even when unseen by others.

 Preparation and materials

- You will need: a small plant in a pot, an ice cream carton, a fizzy drink, a tea towel, an OHP.

 Assembly

1. Show the children your plant. Say that you have just bought it and you are trying to find out the best way to make it grow. Explain that someone said you should feed your plant, so you want to give it some ice cream. Take out the carton and ask the children if you should give it ice cream. Hopefully they will say no!

   Then say that you need to give it a drink, and that you're going to give it fizzy drink. Hopefully the children will stop you. Then say you are sure your plant will be feeling cold and perhaps shy. Try to cover it with a tea towel. Ask the children's opinion and hopefully they will stop you again.

   Just in case you're not told what you're doing wrong, perhaps be ready to say, 'No, I'm sure that's not right', or 'I read somewhere that . . .'

2. Ask the children to tell you what you really need to do: Put the plant in the light, water the plant regularly, give it plant food.

   Write these on the OHP. Say that these are the rules. Are

they good rules? Yes. Why? Because they help the plant to grow.

3. Point out that school rules are similar – they are there to help the school grow into a place where everyone can be happy. God's rules are like that as well – they are there to help all of us grow as people.

4. Tell the following story.

Once there was an emperor in the Far East who was growing old and knew it would soon be time to choose his successor. Instead of choosing one of his assistants or one of his own children, he decided to do something different.

He called all the young people in the kingdom together one day. He said, 'The time has come for me to step down and to choose the next emperor. I have decided to choose one of you.' The kids were shocked! But the emperor continued. 'I am going to give each one of you a seed today – one seed. It is a very special seed. I want you to go home, plant the seed, water it and come back here one year from today with what you have grown from this one seed. I will then judge the plants that you bring to me, and this will tell me who will be the next emperor of the kingdom!'

There was one boy, named Ling, who was there that day and received a seed, along with the others. He went home and excitedly told his mother the whole story. She helped him get a pot and some planting soil, and he planted the seed and watered it carefully. Every day he would water it and watch to see if it had grown.

After about three weeks, a few of the other young people began to talk about their seeds and the plants that were beginning to grow. Ling kept going home and checking his pot, but nothing was growing. Three weeks, four weeks, five weeks went by. Still nothing. By now many others were talking about their plants, but Ling's didn't grow, and he felt like a failure.

Six months went by, and still nothing in Ling's pot. He just knew he had killed his seed. Everyone else had trees and tall plants, but he had nothing. Ling didn't say anything to his friends, however. He just kept waiting for his seed to grow.

Finally a year had passed and all the young people of the

kingdom brought their plants to the emperor for inspection. Ling told his mother that he wasn't going to take an empty pot. But she encouraged him to go, and to take his pot, and to be honest about what happened. Ling felt sick to his stomach, but he knew his mother was right – the emperor had said that they should all return after a year. He took his empty pot to the palace.

When Ling arrived, he was amazed at the variety of plants grown by all the others. They were beautiful, and in all shapes and sizes. Ling put his empty pot on the floor, and many of the others laughed at him. A few felt sorry for him and just said, 'Hey, nice try.'

When the emperor arrived, he surveyed the room and greeted the young people. Ling just tried to hide in the back. 'My, what great plants, trees and flowers you have grown,' said the emperor. 'Today, one of you will be appointed the next emperor!'

All of a sudden, the emperor spotted Ling at the back of the room with his empty pot. He ordered his guards to bring him to the front. Ling was terrified. 'The emperor knows I'm a failure! Maybe he will have me killed!'

When Ling got to the front, the emperor asked his name. 'My name is Ling,' he replied. All the kids were laughing and making fun of him. The emperor asked everyone to quiet down. He looked at Ling, and then announced to the crowd, 'Behold your new emperor! His name is Ling!'

Ling couldn't believe it. Ling couldn't even grow his seed. How could he be the new emperor? Then the emperor said, 'One year ago today, I gave everyone here a seed. I told you to take the seed, plant it, water it, and bring it back to me today. But I gave you all boiled seeds which would not grow. All of you, except Ling, have brought me trees and plants and flowers. When you found that the seed would not grow, you substituted another seed for the one I gave you. Ling was the only one with the courage and honesty to bring me a pot with my seed in it. Therefore, he is the one who will be the new emperor!'

5. Ask the children who kept the emperor's rule. Ling. Was it easy for Ling to stick to the rule? No. It wasn't easy for Ling

to stick to the rule, to do the right thing. He could have cheated and tried to fool everyone. But what counted to the emperor was that Ling kept to the rule even when he thought no one would notice.

6. Say that Christians believe that God sees everything we do and God knows that sometimes it is difficult to do the right thing. If we can be like Ling and stick to what we know is right, then we shall be like plants that grow healthy and tall and strong. Point out that sometimes we're not sure what is right, and then we can talk to people who care for us, like Ling talked to his mother and listened to her advice.

 Time for reflection

Dear God,
Thank you for rules to help us live and grow.
Teach us to do what is right, whether people see what we do or not.
Amen.

 Song

'One more step' (*Come and Praise*, 47)

A TISSUE OF LIES

By the Revd Alan M. Barker

Suitable for Whole School

Aim

To reflect upon the nature of lies.

Preparation and materials

- You will need a toilet roll.
- A colleague should be primed to challenge you (see 2. below).

Assembly

1. Invite the children to recall a word that means 'not telling the truth'. Focus upon the meaning of the words 'lying', 'lies' and 'liar'.

2. Allow a colleague to interject with the challenge: 'Have you ever told a lie?'

    Respond initially by saying, no, of course not. Then apologize and say, yes, of course I have. Reflect further: Haven't most of us told a lie at some time? Perhaps we thought it was only a small lie – and that lying wouldn't do any harm. Maybe that was true, but the trouble with lies is that they can become bigger and stronger than we are.

3. Invite a child or colleague to help demonstrate what you mean. Explain that you are going to tell a story and use some tissue to show how strong lies can become. You could refer to the phrase 'a tissue of lies', saying that it means that lies are often woven together – in other words, more lies are added to the first.

    Ask the helper to hold out their hands together and show how, each time a lie is told, the toilet tissue will be wrapped once around their wrists. Wind a single band and allow the helper to tear through it by pulling their hands apart.

4. Tell the following story, or another of your own making. Invite the children to put up their hands when they think they hear Chloe tell a lie (marked with an asterisk) in the story and each time be ready to wind another layer of tissue around your helper's wrists.

Jessica and Chloe were friends. One day, during playtime, Jessica asked Chloe, 'Will you come to my house to play on Saturday? Mum says you can.'

Chloe didn't really want to. That afternoon she wanted to feel more important than Jessica. 'No, I can't come,' she boasted. 'Dad's promised me a puppy and we're going to get it.'*

It was a lie. Chloe's dad hadn't promised her a puppy, but Jessica didn't know that. She simply said, 'All right then,' and ran off to join some other friends.

'I got out of that one,' thought Chloe. 'Easy!'

(*Allow your helper to break through the single band of tissue.*)

But lying doesn't always make things as easy as you might think. The lie Chloe had told wouldn't go away. (*Start another band of tissue.*)

A few moments later, Adam saw Chloe. 'Jessica told me you're getting a puppy.'

'Yes,'* said Chloe, 'on Saturday*, from the kennels.'*

'Great,' laughed Adam.

Jessica returned. 'You're so lucky. What kind of puppy will it be?'

Chloe thought quickly: 'One of those puppies you see in the TV adverts – a golden one.'*

'Wow! And what will you call it?'

'He's called Goldie.'*

'Can I come with you when you take it for walks?'

'Of course you can,'* said Chloe.

Back in the classroom, it seemed as if everyone had heard! 'Are you getting a puppy?' asked Jade enviously.

'Yes,'* said Chloe again.

'Won't that be fun!' whispered Kevin.

'Yes,'* whispered Chloe.

Chloe enjoyed all the attention. But she knew that what

she'd said wasn't true and secretly she didn't feel very comfortable. She was rather pleased when home-time came.

On Monday morning, Chloe had almost forgotten how she had boasted and told lies to her friends the week before. But when Jessica met her in the playground the first thing that she asked was, 'Did you get your puppy?'

What could Chloe say? There was no puppy. But because she'd lied all her friends thought she had one.

'No,' she said, 'we haven't got the puppy.'

Jessica was surprised: 'Why not?'

Now, Chloe didn't want anyone to know that she'd made up a story that wasn't true and so she continued: 'Because the kennels said it wasn't big enough yet.'* The words tumbled out and Chloe felt awful – the lies seemed so strong that she just couldn't escape from them!

5. Turn to the helper, who will now have nine or more layers of tissue wrapped around their wrists. Add a few more for good measure, commenting how the story shows that lies are so often linked together. Then ask the helper to try to pull their hands apart. This will prove difficult, even impossible! Reflect that one lie may seem a little thing, but that lies can grow and become so strong that we struggle to escape from them.

6. Invite the children to review what they have learned through the story.

 ## Time for reflection

Dear God,
Help us to know the truth,
and to speak the truth,
today and always.
Amen.

 ## Song

'Make me a channel of your peace' (*Come and Praise*, 147)

MY BEST FRIEND

By the Revd Guy Donegan-Cross

Suitable for Whole School

Aim

To explore the giving nature of friendship.

Preparation and materials

- OHP, with acetate sheet with a small rectangle drawn in the middle, and pen.

Assembly

1. Ask the children: Why do we need friends? What do friends do? What are friends like? Consider all responses and, if possible, elicit some examples of good friends and friendly acts. Write one-word summaries of what makes a good friend on the OHP around the rectangle.

2. Tell this story about friendship. (You can act this story out as you tell it.) You might have to explain the word 'grain' or replace it with 'wheat' or 'flour'.

   Two friends worked on a farm collecting grain. Each night they would take their sacks of grain and put them in their stores. One friend was single and lived on his own. The other had a large family. One night the friend with the large family thought, 'This is not fair. My friend lives all on his own and does not enjoy the life of a family. I will help him. I will secretly take one bag of grain and put it in his store at night.' So that night he got one bag out of his store and crept over to his friend's house in the dead of night. He placed the bag in his friend's store and tiptoed home.

   The same night the single friend thought to himself, 'This is not fair. Here am I with only one mouth to feed. My friend, on the other hand, has many children. I think I will take one bag of my grain and secretly put it in his store.' So he took one bag from his store, tiptoed over to his friend's house and placed it in his friend's store.

Every night for weeks the friends would take a bag of grain to each other's stores. But they both became very puzzled, because even though they were giving away their grain the amount they had never seemed to diminish.

One night they were both out carrying sacks of grain to each other's houses. Suddenly they bumped into each other. They looked at each other, saw the bags of grain on their shoulders and suddenly realized what had been happening. They laughed out loud and gave each other a big hug.

Point out that this story shows that true friends give to each other, but also receive.

3. Turn the OHP back on. Ask for suggestions to put in the middle of the rectangle. Can the children suggest some names? (Don't write them in at this stage.) These could be actual people, or generic phrases such as 'best friend', 'my family', perhaps even 'pets', or God or other faith names.

If no one has suggested 'Jesus', write his name in, and say that many people believe they have a special friend who helps them through life. Point out the qualities you have written around the rectangle and apply them to Jesus.

 ## Time for reflection

Dear God,
thank you that you are our friend.
Help us to be friends to each other.
Amen.

 ## Song

'Love is something' (*Come and Praise Beginning*, 16)

CROSSING THE BRIDGE

By Gill O'Neill

Suitable for Whole School

 ### Aim

To present through a play the dilemma of making difficult decisions.

 ### Preparation and materials

- The assembly takes the form of a rehearsed play. You will need eight children to take part.
- You may need to vary the language according to the age of the children.
- The children will need to be familiar with the Three Billy Goats Gruff story.

 ### Assembly

Introduce the play: You have all heard the story of the Three Billy Goats Gruff. They had to go across the bridge to get to the other side. Unfortunately for them, the area under the bridge was inhabited by a very angry Troll. And you'll know how each of the Goats is treated by the Troll, and that finally the Troll meets his match against the biggest of the three Goats. Now meet their grandchildren – or should that be grand kids?

Narrator	One summer, in a paddock not far from here, there was a small herd of kids (baby goats). They had been playing in the same paddock ever since the day that they were born.
Kid 1	What shall we do today?
Kid 2	Why don't we play Hide and Seek?
All	No!
Kid 3	We all know all the hiding places. Not much fun there.

Kid 2	Why don't we climb the hill and find an adventure?
All	No!
Kid 4	We've done that a hundred times before. Boring!
Kid 2	We could always go swimming in the stream.
All	No, too shallow!
Kid 5	That was OK when we were little kids, but the water barely comes up to my knees now.
Kid 2	Why don't we go down to the meadow and have a picnic in the grass?
All	Boring!
Kid 6	We've eaten all the grass there. All that's left is stinging nettles and thistles. Yuck!
Narrator	So the young kids mooched around aimlessly, bumping into each other now and again, and getting on each other's nerves. They'd grown so big that there really wasn't enough room for them in the paddock.

(*All muttering at the same time*)

Kids 1 & 2	I'm bored.
Kid 3	What can we do?
Kid 4	I'm hungry.
Kid 5	This place is too small.
Kid 6	Gerroff, leave me alone.
Narrator	Then one bright spark piped up . . .
Kid 7	I know! Why don't we go across the bridge?
Narrator	A deathly hush descended on the paddock. (*Pause*) The goats stood still, wide-eyed with disbelief. (*Pause*) Eventually they started to speak.
Kid 1	(*obviously fearful*) You know what happened to my cousin, Billy, when he was a kid. He tried to cross the bridge, and the Troll . . . (*sobs, unable to finish*).
Kid 2	Oh yes, and my Nanny, we all know what happened to her!
Kid 7	Yeah, but don't you remember? Granddad Gruff sorted it all out in the end, didn't he? It should be OK now.
Kid 3	How do we know that there's not another Troll under the bridge?
Kid 4	Or something much, much worse?

Kid 5	And what's on the other side anyway?
Kid 6	It'll be too big. The grass will be so long; I'll probably get lost in it. I'm not going over there.
Kid 1	There may be bigger goats. I don't want to go.
Kid 2	If there are other goats, I won't know anyone. I'm not going either.
Kid 3	It's too risky. I don't want to end up in a Troll's burger.
Kid 4	Me neither. Forget it.
Kid 5	I want my Mummy!!
Kid 7	But I thought you were all bored here.
All	WE ARE!
Kid 7	Then we'll have to cross the bridge and see what's there.

(*All goats speak together*)

Kids 1 & 2	But what about the Troll?
Kids 3	But what about the long grass?
Kids 5	But what about the Big Kids?
Kid 7	Maybe if we all stick together we'll be OK. Come on ... I'm going ... Come with me.
All	Oh ... OK.
Narrator	So, led by the little kid, the goats ventured timidly onto the bridge. As they walked across they looked down.
Kid 7	See – there's no sign of any Trolls!!!
All	Phew!
Narrator	This gave them all the confidence they needed. They strode boldly over the rest of the bridge and ran off to find out for themselves what lay beyond. Sometimes they kept together, but eventually ventured out on their own.

 Time for reflection

We all face big changes, big decisions, big steps to take.
Children and staff alike travel into the unknown every day:
will so-and-so make up with me;
how will I do in that test;
will I get that new ... whatever?
And like the Billy Goats we all face difficult decisions:

how can I make it up with my friend;
what should I do about this, that or the other?

Take a moment to think about the things that might come your way and the decisions you might face today.

Like the goats, you'll find it easier to make hard decisions if you make them with friends.

There are good things waiting for you just around the corner. So step out with confidence and take new opportunities in your stride and cross that bridge!

Dear God,
Thank you for the excitement of life,
for new challenges and new steps every day.
Help us to appreciate the opportunities that each day brings.
Thank you for friends and people around us
who can help us to make hard decisions.
Amen.

 Songs

'Travel on' (*Come and Praise*, 42)
'One more step along the world I go' (*Come and Praise*, 47)

ISLAM, RELIGION OF PEACE

By Gordon Lamont

Suitable for KS2

Aim

To think about the roots and essential teaching of Islam.

Preparation and materials

- This assembly will need to be adapted to suit your school situation and experience. In schools with many Muslim children, the material provided will probably be too basic and you may find that the children themselves can present a stronger assembly based on their faith.

Assembly

1. Tell the following story using either these or your own words.

    A long time ago, about 1,500 years ago, a boy was born in a place called Makkah in the country we now know as Saudi Arabia in the Middle East. His was a poor family and his parents were ill. They had both died by the time the boy was just six years old. The boy was then brought up by his grandfather and later his uncle. They were good to the boy and loved him and helped him to start work as a shepherd.

    Later, as he grew into a young man, he began to travel with his uncle. They took long journeys on camels into distant lands, trading goods and meeting people of different tribes. This was an exciting time for the young man, especially when, as he gained experience, he was able to lead the trading journeys himself.

    Later still, when he was a married man, he began to think deeply about his life and what had happened to him. He would go to a lonely cave and wonder how he, once a poor boy with no parents, had become so rich and successful. Yet he did not feel entirely happy and, as he sat in the cave, he suddenly knew why.

The people of Makkah, his home, did not help the poor, they did not look after each other, and they did not feed the hungry or care for the sick. It seemed to him that all they wanted was money and, when they got it, all they wanted was more money! But the more money they had, the less happy they seemed to be.

Then, one day, an extraordinary thing happened. As he sat in the cave thinking these thoughts, an angel appeared before him. This was frightening at first, as you can imagine – it's not the sort of thing that happens every day! The angel said his name was Gabriel and he had a special message – a message from the one true God who the people knew as Allah. So, overcoming his fear, the man in the cave listened to what the angel had to say. Allah wanted all the people to worship only him, the angel said, and they should do this by prayer and saying thank you for all they had, and by helping the poor, the sick, the needy. Allah wanted everyone to try hard to be good and lead honourable lives.

As he heard the angel's words, the man in the cave knew that they were true words – they were just the kind of things he had been thinking about all these years.

The man who had once been a poor boy, then a shepherd, then a merchant, then a thinker, now became a great leader, a prophet – that is, one who speaks God's words. He took the angel's message to the people, a message of faith and belief in one true God, a message of always trying to do your best and caring for the people around you.

This man became so famous that the place where he was born, now named Mecca, has become a place of pilgrimage for people from all over the world and his name is famous too.

2. Ask if anyone knows the name of the man you are describing.

3. When you reveal the name Muhammad, explain that Muslims, followers of his faith, always add 'peace be upon him' after his name when they speak it, as a mark of respect for a very special prophet and his very special message. And

when they write it, they do the same thing by adding (PBUH) after his name.

4. Point out that Islam, the Muslim faith, is now one of the world's great religions and that, like the other major faiths, its main beliefs are about peace and justice, about looking after each other and always seeking to do good.

 Time for reflection

Dear God,
Thank you for the prophet Muhammad – peace be upon him, and all that he taught;
for his care for everyone and his message of peace
and looking after each other.
We thank you for all the good things
that Muslim believers have done through the centuries
as they have tried to put the prophet's words into action.
Whatever our faith, help us to try to be like Muhammad –
 peace be upon him, today;
to do what we can for others,
living in peace with each other.
Amen.

 Song

'When I needed a neighbour' (*Come and Praise*, 65)

ONE STEP AT A TIME

By Gill Hartley

Suitable for Whole School

Aim

To reflect on taking one simple step forward at a time, rather than becoming overwhelmed by difficulties.

Preparation and materials

- A small stepladder, a picture fixed with Blu-Tack to the wall just out of your reach, a set of children's building blocks.
- The assembly includes a number of different examples of how to do things one step at a time. Choose the most appropriate for your children.

Assembly

1. Draw the children's attention to the picture on the wall above you. Demonstrate by jumping that it is too high for you to reach. Move the stepladder and demonstrate that by climbing the first step and then the second you can now reach the picture and remove it from the wall.
2. Ask for a volunteer to start from one side of the room and make their way to the opposite side. Hopefully your volunteer will walk, although try not to use the word 'walk' in your instructions! As she/he does this, ask the children if she/he was able to reach the opposite wall instantly? No, of course not! She/he had to get there by taking one step at a time – another way of describing walking!
3. Ask the children if they know which is the highest mountain in the world. Explain that many people had tried to climb to the summit of Everest before it was finally achieved. On 29 May 1953 Edmund Hillary and his Sherpa guide, Tensing,

finally reached the icy summit. They were the first people to do so and it had been a difficult and exhausting climb to get there.

Does anyone know how high Mount Everest is? Answer: 8,848 metres or 5.5 miles. How do they think Hillary and Tensing managed to climb that high? Did they do it all at once – all in one day? No, it took them many days and they set up camps each time they stopped to rest overnight, all the way up the mountain. They climbed the world's most difficult mountain from camp to camp, one step at a time, until they finally reached the top.

4. Call for some more volunteers. Ask them to build a wall using the children's building blocks. Ask the other children to watch how they do it. When the wall is complete, ask the children watching how the volunteers did it. Emphasize that the wall was built by putting one brick in place at a time. For a bit of fun, ask someone to try building the wall with all the bricks at once!

5. Ask if anyone knows the name of the most famous city in the Roman Empire. Tell them that there is a famous saying (or proverb): Rome was not built in a day. What do they think this means? Literally it means that the town was too big to build in one day, but the proverb has now come to mean that anything difficult cannot be done all at once, it has to be done a bit (or a step) at a time.

6. Ask the children to tell you about how they write a story. Hopefully you may find someone who mentions a beginning, a middle and an end! Use this to further illustrate the point that difficult tasks cannot be achieved instantly, they take time and have to be tackled one section (or step) at a time.

7. Ask the children to close their eyes and imagine:

Your teacher asks you and your friend to clean up the paint cupboard (or substitute if you don't have one!). You open the doors and look inside. The shelves are full of pots and brushes and mixing trays all covered with paint. You panic! You'll never get it all done by home time! As you stand there wondering what to do, your friend says, 'Let's collect up all the mixing trays and wash them first.' Together you do that and leave them to dry.

After that, you suggest taking out all the paint pots to wash. You leave them to dry as well. That only leaves the brushes. Your friend passes them to you and you wash them. By now the mixing trays and paint pots are dry and you can put them back into the cupboard. You put the brushes into a jar and close the cupboard door.

The bell rings. It's home time, and you've finished! You didn't think you would finish in time! How much easier it is when you do one bit at a time!

Time for reflection

Dear God,
Help us when we have to do something hard.
Help us to see what needs to be done first.
Keep us calm to work out what needs to be done next.
Give us patience to keep going on to the next step.
Help us to keep going to the end, until it is finished and we
can enjoy our success.
Amen.

Song

'All over the world' (*Come and Praise*, 61)

BEING MYSELF

By the Revd Alan M. Barker and Laura Barker

Suitable for KS1

Aim

To celebrate our God-given individuality.

Preparation and materials

- You will need four (or more) teddy bears of contrasting character. (This could be your opportunity to support your local charity shops!)

Assembly

1. Introduce the bears to the children, one by one. Invite them to say something about each one, e.g. Is this bear big or small? Young or old? A boy or girl bear? Is this bear a happy bear or a grumpy bear? A noisy bear or a quiet bear? A bear who likes to be on its own or with others? A bear that likes to run and jump or one that likes to sleep? What does this bear like to eat when it goes to the teddy bears' picnic? What does this bear like to wear? Can you think of a name for this bear?

2. Point out that no two of the teddy bears are quite the same. Each one is different. Ask the children to consider which bear they would most like to be friends with. Why?

3. Invite the children to reflect upon their different choices. Like the bears, we are all different. We each look different. We are of various ages and all have different birthdays. We like doing different things. We each have our own name.

4. Was having to choose just one bear difficult? Who would have wanted to be friends with all the bears? Share the thought that, like the bears, everyone is different, but God chooses to be friends with all of us. We are 'children of God', which

means that although we are all different, each one of us is special.

Time for reflection

Invite the children quietly to look around at one another as you say this prayer:

'We are children of God' (Romans 8.16)

Lord God,
Thank you for the different ways
in which we are each special.
Together we belong to your family.
Help us to care for one another
as you care for us all.
Amen.

Song

'He's got the whole world in his hands' (*Come and Praise*, 19)

SMELLY SOCKS

By the Revd Alan M. Barker

Suitable for KS1/Whole School

 Aim

To appreciate the importance of, and celebrate, our sense of smell.

 Preparation and materials

- You will need a number of items with characteristic fragrance or odour, e.g. a scented rose, lavender, mint leaves, orange peel or banana skin, a strong-smelling sweet, freshly baked bread, shoe or furniture polish, a newly printed magazine.
- Also a sock washed using fabric conditioner.

 Assembly

1. Invite a number of children to come forward, and to close their eyes while smelling the items. Ask them to identify what they can smell. Have fun with the sock, which should be introduced last of all. Point out that some smells are pleasant, while others are not. Socks can be horribly smelly!
2. Reflect that our sense of smell can add to our enjoyment of being alive. What smells do the children remember and like? Does the school have any distinctive smells? Are there any special 'summer' smells? e.g. newly cut grass, hot tar on the pavement, blossom and flowers, strawberries!
3. Point out that while many smells are attractive (e.g. cooking food), some are unpleasant (e.g. the smell of food that has gone bad). Smells can also warn us of danger, e.g. the smell of burning if the food is left too long on the cooker.
4. Explain that many creatures have a keener sense of smell than human beings. Specially trained police dogs can track and

sniff out people who are lost or hiding. Their noses are different from ours.

5. Encourage the children to be more aware of their sense of smell and to be thankful for it. Explain that you're going to teach them a special song about this.

Fun song: Smelly Socks
These words may be sung to the tune of 'Thank you Lord for this fine day' (*Come and Praise*, 32), with a pause in the fourth line for the imaginary smells to be sniffed and the final response spoken.

Can you smell the scented flowers?
Can you smell the scented flowers?
Can you smell the scented flowers?
(*sniff*) Aah!

Can you smell the baking bread? (*three times*)
(*sniff*) Yum, yum!

Can you smell the burning toast? (*three times*)
(*sniff*) Oops!

Can you smell Dad's smelly socks? (*three times*)
(*sniff*) Ugh!!

Let's all get some clean fresh air (*three times*)
(*deep breath*) That's better!

 Time for reflection

Explain that the words 'fragrance', 'aroma' and 'scent' are all used to describe smells.

Creator God,
Thank you for our noses
and the many different things that we can smell.
For familiar fragrances that we know well
and for new scents and aromas that excite our senses.
Amen.

Indexes

Index of Authors

Index of Biblical References

Index of Themes and Content

Actions/activity

Bible

Drama

KS1

KS2

Seasonal

Advent 12; The birthday of Guru Nanak (Sikh) 99; Bodhi Day (Buddhist) 106; Chinese New Year or Yuan Tan 111; Divali (Hindu) 80; Epiphany 22; The flying pizza 3; Ganesh-Chaturthi (Hindu) 73; Getting stirred up! 9; Hanukah (Jewish) 96; Holi (Hindu) 77; The prophet's night journey and ascension (Muslim) 83; Ramadan (Muslim) 87; Remembering together 6; Ridvan (Baha'i) 114; Rosh Hashana (Jewish) 90; Sukkot (Jewish) 93; Vaisakhi (Sikh) 102

Story presentation

Actions speak louder than words 53; The birthday of Guru Nanak (Sikh) 99; Bodhi Day (Buddhist) 106; A camel through the eye of a needle 39; Caring for God's creatures 24; Divali (Hindu) 80; 'Feely' fingers 63; Ganesh-Chaturthi (Hindu) 73; Hanukah (Jewish) 96; Holi (Hindu) 77; Islam, religion of peace 142; The legend of St Boniface 15; The lost coin 60; Mary's story 31; My best friend 136; Noah and his ark 43; Noah and the flood 47; Noah and the rainbow 50; Peace 58; The prophet's

night journey and ascension (Muslim) 83; Ramadan (Muslim) 87; Rosh Hashana (Jewish) 90; Rules for life 129; The shepherd's story 19; The sixth word 37; Sukkot (Jewish) 93; A tissue of lies 133; True supporters 27; Vaisakhi (Sikh) 102; Water of life 125

Whole school

Actions speak louder than words 53; Advent 12; Crossing the bridge 138; Divali (Hindu) 80; Epiphany 22; 'Feely' fingers 63; The flying pizza 3; Ganesh-Chaturthi (Hindu) 73; Getting stirred up! 9; The goose with the golden eggs 119; Hanukah (Jewish) 96; Holi (Hindu) 77; The lost coin 60; Mary's story 31; My best friend 136; Noah and his ark 43; Noah and the flood 47; Noah and the rainbow 50; One step at a time 145; Peace 58; The prophet's night journey and ascension (Muslim) 83; Ridvan (Baha'i) 114; Rosh Hashana (Jewish) 90; Rules for life 129; The shepherd's story 19; The sixth word 37; Sukkot (Jewish) 93; The sun and the wind 122; A tissue of lies 133; The unforgiving servant 66; Vaisakhi (Sikh) 102; Water of life 125